IT'S YOUR TURN TO GET RICH!

by

Adam J. Lear

Copyright © 1984 Adam J. Lear

All rights reserved. This book, or any part thereof, may not be reproduced in whole or in part without permission in writing from publisher.

Publisher by:
New Start Publications, Inc.
100 Glenn Drive
Sterling, Virginia 22170

Printed in the United States of America

TABLE OF CONTENTS

1. The $85.000.00 Weekend Special Event..................1
2. The "Used Automobile" Shortcut To $65,000 A Year!.......15
3. The Golden $50,000 Dollar Bonanza..................19
4. Wholesaling Your Way To $72,000 A Year!....................28
5. Twelve Hours Of Fun — To Make $3,000 Or $10,000 In Profits...44
6. A $500,000 A Year Business With Little Or No Investment!53
7. Start Your Own Company For A Song And Make $3,000 A Month For Singing..60
8. Rent-A-Game And Make $68,000 The First Year.............71
9. How To Start A "Bargain Business" And Make Over $390,000 The First Year..82
10. $25,000 In Six Weeks Is Hard To Beat!..........................94
11. Sit At Home — And Earn $100,000 Annually!................105
12. Quick Relief For Your Money Problems.......................148

FOR ADDITIONAL FREE BROCHURES ON OTHER BOOKS AVAILABLE FROM NEW START PUBLICATIONS

For free brochures containing detailed information and discriptions of titles available write us. They are free for the asking.
To receive them, simply select your book of interest and write the title of book and code number and send it to the address below.

The Get Report
by Robert Shindler
CODE A-1

Shortcuts To Becoming Rich
by Robert Shindler
CODE B-2

How To Get By On $10,000 A Day!
by Debra Grubbs
CODE C-3

$25,000 Dollars For A Few Hours Work Doesn't Seem Fair!
by John Chriswell
CODE D-4

The Crandall Secret
by Daniel A. Crandall
CODE E-5

A Oppportunity To Get Rich In Your Own Mail Order Business.
by John Chriswell
(Because of the size of this large 24 inch package please include **$1 dollar** *to defray the cost of postage.) Thank You!*

For your Free Brochures write to:
John Shumway
Mail Order Sales
NEW START PUBLICATIONS
100 Glenn Drive
P.O. Box 139
Sterling, Virginia 22170

CHAPTER ONE

THE $85,000.00 WEEKEND SPECIAL EVENT.

If you want to make $25,000 to $85,000 for one weekend's work, then this chapter will definitely interest you.

I am not going to use up space in this chapter telling you about the success stories of Seminar Promoters of the past. You already know, or probably heard, about how a Seminar can earn a promoter up to $85,000.00 for one weekend's work.

Let's Get Right To The Subject At Hand! "$85,000." And How To Make It.

The key to putting a Seminar together, and perhaps earning $85,000 for three days' work, is to:
1. Locate the right location, preferably in a major city.
2. Find and hire the right speakers.
3. And, last but not least, induce lots of people to send in $450 dollars each.

Let's take the planning of a seminar from stage one to the final production in a step-by-step manner.

The first step requires no money—only thinking on your part. Here are some of the questions that you must ask yourself.

Pick Out A Subject. Let's take Mail-Order self-publishing. "This shouldn't be too difficult."

There are probably about 100 people in the country qualified to participate in a seminar on mail-order self-publishing. I'll show you how to find them.

Decide on who your speakers will be. You must know how many speakers you are going to hire and how much you are going to pay them. Break down the seminar into two days and then into four sessions per day, two hours per speaker. Then decide who among the list of qualified speakers is best qualified to teach each session. You don't have to call the speakers this very minute, but it's not a bad idea to talk to them on a preliminary basis. ★ I'll list a source at the end of this chapter for speakers on various subjects.

Select the dates and location for your seminar. You need this information to budget for travel and hotel expenses. Let's say you are going to hold your first seminar in Dallas, Texas, then you are going to need to know the cost of hotel accommodations and dates the hotel will be available to accommodate—at least 300 to 400 people.

Estimate the amount of attendance. This step is part guess work and part common sense. Let's assume that the amount of people who are interested in Mail-Order Self-Publishing within 2000 miles of Dallas is 75,000. Once you have selected 75,000 potential names, you can reasonably expect to pull a response of .37 percent, or 278 attendees.

Select a registration fee. Ask your next-store neighbor, ask a fortune teller, or look at your competition. The registration fee should be high enough or everyone will think it isn't worth the trip.

Let's say you chose $450, that's what everyone in the business feels the market will bear for a two-day seminar.

Calculate your gross income from your two-day seminar. This is fun: 278 attendees times $450 is $125,100.

Calculate your expenses. Per each attendee: Books and materials $10. Lunches, two days $16. Coffee breaks $6. = Total $32.00. Leaving $418 gross profit.

Calculate your Speaker Fees. Here's were you may come out way ahead. Some speakers will be glad to speak at your seminar for the exposure; no charge. They really want exposure for their books, cassette tapes, etc. They make a nice profit from this back-end business, and in some cases would be more than happy to speak at your seminar FREE OF CHARGE. But we can't rely on this happening in all cases, if it does, all the better. But, for illustration purposes let's don't rely on it happening at all.

Calculating the cost of speakers can range from $500 for one hour to $5,000 for all day. The way we usually estimate this cost is $1,500 per speaker for a two-hour session. Four sessions per day equals $6,000 per day or $12,000 for two days.

Travel and hotel expenses. Air travel, room and board for one speaker and one staff member. "Usually his wife." $1,800.

Travel expenses, room and board for you and four staff members. $5,000.

Total expenses for eight speakers and their staff members $14,400. Plus $5,000 for yourself and your four staff members.
Total cost $19,400.
Here's how it breaks down:
278 attendees at $450 is $125,100.
Expenses for 278 attendees, books, materials, coffee breaks, etc. is $8,900.
Expenses for speakers, staff members, and yourself $31,400
YOUR NET PROFIT for one weekend's work $84,800.00.

Not bad for a few days' work, besides you can hold the seminar anywhere you desire. Just think of an interesting resort you would like to visit, anywhere in the world and hold your next seminar there. "Now lets seeeee... Hawaii; Hong Kong; Stutgart, Germany; London, England or perhaps even Paris, France.

Enough of all that, let's get back to business. Next is Calculating Start Up Expenses.

Calculate start up expenses.

1. Designing a four-page brochure $500 to $1,000.

2. Print and mail to 75,000 people: 16 cents each or roughly, $1,200.

3. Cost for people to design, write promotional copy: $500.

4. Miscellaneous expenses, including long distance telephone calls: $500.

PREPARING FOR THE SEMINAR.

As a general rule, the promotional mailing should go out 11 weeks prior to the seminar. The seminar itself requires time and effort on your part. Right from the beginning you should structure each program so speakers and attendees alike know where and when each session starts and finishes. This is not hard to organize but some time and thought should be given to each phase of your first seminar. Starting with the air plane landing in Dallas, transporation to and from the air port. Relaxing diversions for your attendees, (night life, restaurants, and entertainment centers.)

There are several ways to accomplish this: You could hire a seminar consultant and pay him 10 percent of your net profit. Or you can do it yourself. I recommend the latter. It is far cheaper and once you have your complete plan outlined on paper, everything will start to fall into place.

LECTURE BUREAUS

There are several speakers bureaus located in the New York area that will be glad to provide you with speakers of all types. Entertainment, sports, finaicial, sales motivators, banking, real estate, mail order, direct marketing, magazine publishing, book publishing, etc.

Enterprises Unlimited
59th & 1st Avenue
New York, N. Y. 10017

International Stock Exchange Information Bureau
120 Wall Street
New York N.Y. 10002

Leigh Bureau
Entertainers
Lectures
49-51 State Road
Princeton, N.J. 08711

Program Corporation Of America
Leading Speakers
Performing Artists
Special Events Programs
Conventions
595 W. Hartsdale Avenue
White Plains, N.Y. 10607

Charles Rothschild Productions
330 E 48th Street
New York, N.Y. 10020

Ruth Szold Promotional Models
644 Broadway
New York, N.Y. 10020

Leonard Gladstone Variety Lectures
1039 Franklin Avenue
Valley Stream, N.Y. 10980

By expanding the plan you can hold several different seminars on different subjects throughout the year. Your investment is the cost of the brochure and the mailing list. If at first you don't succeed try again with another subject. Try Real Estate for example. That will surely become a sought after seminar in the coming months. Real Estate will be coming back strong prior to the next presidental election, and believe me, this type of seminar will be in great demand.

Mailing lists can be recommended and purchased through recognized Mailing List Brokers. Here are a few that specialize in seminars:

AZ Lists, Inc.
270 Mason St.
Greenwich, CT 06830

Abelow Response Inc.
430 W. Merrick Rd.
Valley Stream, NY 11580

Accredited Mailing Lists, Inc.
3 Park Ave
New York, NY 10016

Advanced Management Systems, Inc.
9225 Sunset Blvd., Penthouse
Los Angeles, CA 90069

American Mailing Lists Corp.
7777 Leesburg Pike
Falls Church, VA 22043

George Bryant & Staff
71 Grand Ave.
Englewood, NJ 07631

Bernice Bush Company
15052 Springdale St., Ste. A
Huntington Beach, CA 92649

Celco
381 Park Ave. South, Ste. 919
New York, NY 10016

Concepts for Children, Inc.
607 Palisade Ave.
Englewood Cliffs, NJ 07632

Consumer's Advertising &
Marketing Associates, Inc. (Canada)
P.O. Box 930
Hightstown, NJ 08520

The Coolidge Company
25 West 43rd St.
New York, NY 10036

Charles Crane Associates Corp.
1 Executive Drive
Fort Lee, NJ 07024

Custom List Services, Inc.
Three Metro Plaza, Ste. 107
8300 Professional Pl.
Landover, MD 20785

D-J Associates
Route 22, Box 517
Croton Falls, NY 10519

D-J Associates
P.O. Box 217
Center Conway, NH 03813

Dependable Lists, Inc.
33 Irving Place
New York, NY 10003

Dependable Lists, Inc.
333 N. Michigan Ave.
Chicago, IL 60601

Dependable Lists, Inc.
1825 K St., N.W.
Washington, DC 20006

Direct Media, Inc.
90 S. Ridge St.
Port Chester, NY 10573

Direct Media, Inc.
310 Madison Ave., Room 1717
New York, NY 10017

Direct Media, Inc.
3414 S. Broadway
Edmond, OK 73034

Direct Media, Inc.
406 Chestnut Lane
Wayne, PA 19087

Dominion Mail Mktg. Consultants
4800 Cote des Neiges
Montreal, Que., Canada H3V 1G2

Alan Drey Company, Inc.
600 Third Ave.
New York, NY 10016

Alan Drey Company, Inc.
333 N. Michigan Ave.
Chicago, IL 60601

Carol Enters List Co., Inc.
381 Park Ave. So., Ste. 919
New York, NY 10016

Saul Gale Assoc., Inc.
57-03 Kissena Blvd.
Flushing, NY 11355

An opportunity like this may sound too good to be true, but it's not.

The opportunity exists in the arena of Seminars—an exciting, fast paced, high profit field where you can leverage your small investment and creativity—into $85,000.00 quickly!

Seminars will give you the spectacular profit potential of the most highly lucrative business imaginable without a lot of risk taking.

The reason Seminars are becoming so popular is because it gives the middle-income entrepreneur an opportunity to make staggering profits without actually investing heavily. No office to rent. No inventory to purchase. No Equipment to worry about. No large headaches, whatsoever!

Unlike any other business I know of you can earn tens of thousands and, on some occasions, even hundreds of thousands of dollars without being on the hook for more than just pocket money. And besides, Seminars are the only area of business I know of where you can reap spectacular rewards from somebody eles's work.

Consider This Fact:

★ You can begin with only $500-$1000 out of pocket investment yet earn the profits from a single seminar in the $45,000-$85,000 range or higher.

In summary, it's an ideal method for anyone who wants a high profit potential, but hassle-free income every month from creative Seminars.

Of course, just like any other business it does have a few risks. But paradoxically, I think you'll see the risk element of Seminars is perhaps much less than the average mom and pop type operation. The risk is that you can lose a modest amount of time and money (something remarkably few entrepreneurs are willing to invest) if a specific Seminar fails to materialize, but that's your only loss. The advantage is that you cannot lose a penny more.

Seminars offer many of the dynamic profit potentials of say, Mail-Order Retailing, without that level of risk.

Seminars can give you such powerful leverage (in general between 10 to 1 and 20 to 1 or better) that it can enable you to turn a relatively modest investment, and a little time and effort into a small fortune.

One of the best features of Seminars is that you don't need any real starting capital to speak of. You can begin with as little as five hundred to a thousand dollars. In just one seminar my colleague used less than this to make a clear profit of $80,000.

You can do this quietly and discreetly without quitting your job or disrupting your other business activities.

You don't need any elaborate experience or skill—just a desire to profit and the willingness to learn. Giving a Seminar is actually a simple and exciting field that can be mastered by following a few simple rules I have laid out in this chapter.

Good Luck and I hope to see you in perhaps Los Angles, Dallas, Hawaii, or perhaps even London, England.

The following is an example of what a Seminar (mail-out) Brochure should look like:

Mark O. Haroldsen Invites You To

Atlantic City

October 11th-14th

The
Eastern National
Real Estate Investor's

Convention

Join Investors from all over the country at the beautiful Playboy Resort Hotel for The National Real Estate Investor Convention for Only $119.95.

"Spend 4 Full days of intensive training by the best real estate investors in the country. Learn new techniques that will make you wealthy."

Mark O. Haroldsen

Learn From The Nation's Top Experts How To:

- Take Advantage of the Coming "New Real Estate Boom"
- How to Take Advantage of Current Low Interest Rates
- Use the Newest No Money Down Techniques
- Legally Cut Your Income Tax to Zero
- Negotiate and Save Thousands of Dollars
- Use Paper Instead of Money
- Make a Fortune in Rehabs
- Form Profitable Syndications
- Become Wealthy Through Foreclosures
- To Form Partnerships
- Create Cash Flow through Government Loans

And 20 Other Topics

The Best Educational Experience Anywhere

I recently returned from our convention in Dallas and sat down in my office to read the evaluation sheets. I was very pleased as 95% of the attendees rated the convention "excellent." It makes me feel very good to see people take the fantastic knowledge that is available at the convention and put it into practice.

When people tell me they put $100,000 in their pocket from a few ideas they got at the previous convention 6 months ago, I know we are doing something right. I looked at an evaluation sheet and under comments and suggestions I read; "I have been to numerous architect, landscape, CPA and medical conventions, but this was the best organized, informative, hospitable, helpful, reasonably priced convention I have ever attended anywhere. Hurrah for you guys for organizing and putting this on!"

Mark O. Haroldsen

This is the best real estate program in the United States today. We are very proud and happy that we can help people better their lives. Look at this brochure carefully — don't think this is just another seminar — I promise you it isn't. This may be the opportunity to really get you going on the road to *your* financial freedom.

131 Years of Real Estate Experience

We are told the best teacher in life is experience. The men and women you see in the brochure have accumulated over 131 years of real estate experience. You can learn from the mistakes and successes of these men.

Gordon Walker Pete Blazer Steve Thomas Dave Shamy Phil Drummond Wade Cook

J.C. Ebach Barney Zick Jimmy Napier Wayne Phillips Joe Land Thompson-Sulenberger

Dick Lee James M. Dykes Dave Deebach Mark O. Haroldsen Billy Burden Bob Harrington

Four Days That Will Propel You Ahead in Your Life

A rudderless ship will always head off in an unknown direction and arrive at an unknown destination. Many times it will go in circles and get nowhere. Many of us are like a rudderless ship, our engine is tuned and willing to do the work but we lack the knowledge or direction to propel us forward. We work hard but end up going in circles.

A Small Price to Pay for Success

If your future — your happiness — your self-fulfillment mean anything to you, you can't afford to miss this convention. Compare this with other seminars or conventions and see how we stack up.

- 4 Days of Instruction
- 16 Nationally Famous Real Estate Experts
- 24 Hours of Instruction
- Nation's Largest Real Estate Bookstore
- Low Price of $119.95
- Expenses to Convention Tax Deductible
- Hundreds of Investors from Your Area
- The Top Real Estate Experts in U.S. today
- 62 Unique 2 hr Sessions

Why Should I Go?

Real estate has been and still is the safest, fastest and most lucrative investment available. If you want to obtain financial freedom and you are not afraid of some hard work, we will give you the direction you need to obtain that freedom. Today's investors must utilize the newest techniques. This convention is geared to teach the methods that are working today. Real estate sales people and brokers will find classes especially geared to their needs. You will find this convention invaluable.

What Will I Get Out of It?

Our convention format is a time tested program designed to give the broadest and most valuable instruction in the area of real estate. You plan your own schedule picking the classes that most apply to your personal needs. Classes are structured to be small enough to answer questions and problems. Major speakers are scheduled to address the convention as a whole. Plenty of time is allotted to get to know other investors from your area and from across the country.

How Will I Benefit?

We offer a money back guarantee. Of the 14,000 people who have attended our past conventions, only 12 people have asked for a refund. At the convention you will be exposed to new ideas and methods. You will be refreshed on the basics and thoroughly motivated to go home and start making money. In one room you will find thousands of books and tapes covering every aspect of real estate. This is the greatest collection of real estate educational knowledge assembled anywhere in the U.S.

How Do I Sign Up?

Fill out the registration form on the back page. *Please Print Clearly* — Send a check or credit card information, in a few weeks we will send you a confirmation. You may call direct at 801-943-1280 with credit card information and register over the phone.

SPECIAL GUEST SPEAKER
Senator Jake Garn

Prior to his election to the Senate in 1974, Senator Garn served on the Salt Lake City Commission for four years and was elected Mayor in 1971. He was active in the Utah League of Cities and Towns and served as President in 1972. In 1974, he was First Vice President of the National League of Cities and served as Honorary President in 1975.

Senator Garn was elected to a second term in the Senate in November, 1980. He received 74 percent of the vote, the largest victory in a statewide race in Utah history.

Senator Garn is chairman of the Senate Banking, Housing and Urban Affairs Committee and serves on three subcommittees: Housing and Urban Affairs; Financial Institutions; and International Finance and Monetary Policy. The senior Utah Senator also is a member of the Senate Appropriations Committee and serves as chairman of the HUD-Independent Agencies Subcommittee. He serves on four other Appropriations subcommittees: Energy and Water Resources; Denfense; Military Construction; and Interior. He serves on the Senate Committee on Intelligene and has four subcommittee assignments: Budget; Analysis and Production; Legislation and the Rights of Americans; and Collection and Foreign Operations.

Senator Garn was unanimously reelected to a leadership position in the Senate as Secretary of the Republican Conference for the 98th Congress.

Jake Garn

Make Your Atlantic City Trip Tax Deductible:

Deduction: Treasury Regulation 1-162-5 permits an income tax deduction for educational expenses (registration fees, cost of travel, meals and lodging) undertaken to maintain or improve skills required in one's employment or other trade or business. The IRS recommends you keep a daily record of expenditures in accordance with this regulation.

Special Room Discount at the Playboy Hotel and Casino

Discount Rate $65.00 per night*
Single or Double Occupancy
*Discount from Normal Rate

Playboy Hotel and Casino
2500 Boardwalk
Atlantic City, NJ 08404
609-344-4000 or 800-257-8672
In New Jersey 800-582-7040

Don't wait to make room reservations – Do it today. All blocked rooms will be released September 10. If you phone, mention you are with Mark O. Haroldsen's Real Estate Investors Convention for room discount.

Convention Format and Schedule
Registration - Tuesday Oct 11 Noon-6:00 p.m.
First Session will begin Oct 11 at 6:00 p.m
Convention Conclusion - Friday Oct 14 at 3:00 p.m.
No Smoking or Tape Recording

NIFP reserves the right to substitute speakers due to unforseeable circumstances.
You are responsible for your own hotel reservations.
Fill Out and Mail This Form Today To:

1983 Investor's Convention – Atlantic City
1831 Fort Union Blvd.
Salt Lake City, Utah 84121
or call (801) 943-1280

Convention Fee:
$119.95 per person, if you register before Sept 19
$139.95 per person, if you register after Sept 19
Cancellations: Full refund of convention fee if notified prior to Sept 23. If notified after Sept 23 you are eligible for a raincheck, not a refund.

Registration Form

Bulk Rate
U.S. Postage
PAID
Salt Lake City, Utah
Permit No. 1122

Participants:

1. _____
   Name (as you would like printed on name tag)   phone no.
   _____
   Address   City, State, Zip

2. _____
   Name (as you would like printed on name tag)   phone no.
   _____
   Address   City, State, Zip

3. _____
   Name (as you would like printed on name tag)   phone no.
   _____
   Address   City, State, Zip

Method of Payment:
Total Due: $_____ must be paid in full!
[ ] Check enclosed   [ ] Visa   [ ] Mastercard   [ ] American Express   [ ] Other
Credit Card No. _____   Exp. Date _____

Office Use Only:
Da R ___   Appr ___   Ch No ___   Am ___

CHAPTER TWO

THE "USED AUTOMOBILE" SHORTCUT TO $65,000 A YEAR!

Since the automobile was invented, in 1908, entrepreneurs and businessmen from one end of the country to the other have sold it, raced it, rented it, leased it, treasured it, and resold it again.

But, no one has ever come up with the idea to: "Lease It Used."

My idea is simple!

Step One: Subscribe to the used car dealers bible: "The Black Book," $52 a year for 52 issues, address: National Auto Research, P.O. Box 758, Gainesville, Georgia 30503. Telephone: (404) 532-4111.

Make sure you tell them you are starting a Used-Car-Business, and what STATE you reside in, or they won't let you subscribe to it.

Step Two: Proceed to your local "Department of Motor Vehicles," and apply for a used car dealers license.

Step Three: Purchase two cars from your local "Wholesale Automobile Auction." (The Back Book will tell you where they are located in your part of the country.) Pay no more than $200 for each car and make sure they are in good running condition.

Step Four: Stop by your local NEW Car leasing company and obtain a copy of their Leasing Agreement. Change it to fit your new business, have a typesetter reset it, and have 200 printed at your local Quick-Print-Shop.

Step Five: Run an advertisement in your local paper as follows:

LEASE A USED CAR
Lincoln Continental, 4dr, PS, PB, Air, Automatic, Sunroof, Stereo Radio, loaded. $95 per month. 6-month lease.
No Credit Check.
United Leasing Company
200 University Blvd.
Silver Spring, Maryland 20077
Phone 555-1012

Here's how the plan works:

Collect from your customer the first month's lease payment ($95) plus a $100 security deposit. ($195.) Have him or her sign a six-month renewable (open end) lease.

As you can readily see, you have already received your $200 investment back, less the cost of advertising. Once you have leased your second car you will be even.

Now comes the profit picture. "Boy this is fun!" $95 per month times 5 months = $475. Times two cars = $950. "Do you realize you are now receiving $190 a month for doing nothing?"

Step Six: Go back to the "Automobile Auction," with the same $400 you started with, and repeat the process over again until you are making $190 every two weeks, then $190 every week and then $190 a day.

Start Building your business, by purchasing two cars per week until you have 25 cars on the road.

As your customers turn in the cars, at the end of their lease, take them back to the auction and sell them for $75 to $100. *You see, a used car almost never goes below $100 wholesale—unless it doesn't run, then the junk dealer may give you $25 for it.*

Don't forget your customers will most likely want to lease another car from you, when their six months are up. So, in most cases, you will never have to give back the $100 security deposit. Just put them into one of your *New* used cars on your lot and start the process all over again.

Depending on how much money you want to make, this business could easily build up to $64,000 a year, starting with just a $500 dollar investment.

P.S. Customers always pay for their own insurance.

P.P.S. Also, it is not necessary for you to start your own "Used Car Business" with a dealers license from the state.
I just suggested that step so you would enjoy a little more flexibility.

IF YOU'RE TIRED OF THE RAT RACE

CHAPTER THREE

THE GOLDEN $50,000 DOLLAR BONANZA

Everyone knows gold is the most highly valued metal on Earth. But if you've ever thought about going into the business of buying and selling gold, you might be surprised to learn how little it will cost you to cash in on the worldwide obsession with the glittering metal.

The capital requirement to start a small-scale gold dealership could be as little as $5,000, according to dealers already in the business. "You need some basic knowledge and a little equipment," said Salem David, owner of the Louisiana Gold and Silver Shop. "The cost to start this business is minimal."

Gold prices began to rise from historically low levels in the 70s, but the "New Gold Rush" began in earnest when the U.S. legalized private ownership of gold in 1975. After years of fantastic increases, the price of gold has stabilized at the $400 per ounce range.

But the demand for gold remains strong while the supply is limited. In addition to its attraction as an investment, it's used for jewelry and industrial purposes. The price might not be as high as it has been, but there is always a market for a dealer with gold to sell.

Most gold dealers say they make a comfortable living from their businesses, although their profits obviously depend on the scale of their operation and market conditions. Assuming a margin of roughly 20 percent between the price a dealer pays and the price he receives, a small scale operator can expect to clear anywhere from $35,000 to $50,000 a year.

But most dealers don't deal in gold exclusively. In most cases, they also handle silver, other precious metals and gems. Many shop owners also buy and sell coins or jewelry.

Although gems and coins require special expertise, an entrepreneur who is set up to deal in gold can expand his business to deal in silver and other precious metals fairly easily.

The first step in setting up such a business is to check the applicable state and local laws, since trading in gold is heavily regulated, In most cases, dealers must be licensed and must indicate their business address to get a license. So, if you don't want to lose your security deposit and first month's rent, you should be sure you meet the applicable licensing requirements before renting a shop. *(They are not that strict almost anyone can qualify for a license.)*

Once you've rented a shop and complied with the law, it's a simple matter to start buying and selling gold. Like any business, you need some furniture, a phone, a sign, and an ad in the Yellow Pages. Only two special pieces of equipment are needed—a testing kit to evaluate the gold you buy and a scale to weigh it.

"Testing equipment is very important," said the owner of a gold dealership in Alexandria, Va. "If you're not careful with it, you can buy a lot of bad merchandise." That equipment includes nitric and hydrochloric acid and tools to apply the acids to gold, all for less than $50.

Next, you need a scale for weighing gold that is calibrated by pennyweights, a unit of measurement for Troy weight, which is used for gold and other precious metals. The scales cost around $200 each, and you may want to have two in case one breaks or if you hire another employee.

Although it's possible to minimize the risk of theft by shipping gold to buyer as often as possible, many dealers also invest in security precautions ranging from a safe or burglar alarm to guns.

You can do it all for as little as $5,000, assuming you can buy equipment and pay your overhead and still have a few thousand dollars to buy gold. Of course, you can also spend much more, especially if you want to buy more gold to increase your volume.

There are also trade-offs to be made. For instance, most dealers are happy to spend more money to rent a shop in a prime location with a lot of activity. In the long run, it saves them money on advertising and security because their shop is readily visible to customers and police alike.

"You need a prime location on a corner," said the Alexandria shop owner. "A second class location means a second class living. If you save money on rent, you'll lose 10 times that in profits."

Newcomers to the gold business must also decide whether they want to sell the scrap gold they buy on an as-is basis or start their own refining operation. Gold which has been refined into its pure state (24 karat gold) brings a higher price when resold. On the other hand, setting up a small refining operation will cost at least $15,000 and require special skills.

Once you have established the scope of your business and set up shop, you're ready to start buying gold. If you go into refining, you might buy gold from jewelry stores or manufacturers, or from pawn shops. If you plan to sell scrap on an as-is basis, you will have to buy from the public primarily.

Depending on the market and how much you advertise, the public will offer you everything from old jewelry to gold teeth. But if you're buying from the public, you have to be prepared to hold each and every piece you buy for as long as 15 to 30 days before reselling it.

In most places, state or local law mandates a holding period and paperwork requirements so the police can intercept stolen merchandise. Obviously, that ties up your investment until the holding period is over.

The amount and timing of your eventual return on that investment will depend on wether you sell your gold after the holding period ends. A large refiner will pay 98 percent or 99 percent of the market price, but only after refining the gold and/or testing the refined product, a process that can take up to 30 days.

During that period, the price might drop from the point at which you bought the gold, reducing or wiping out your profit. In addition, refiners will charge fees for the refining and assay processes, making it uneconomical to sell them small amounts of gold.

On the other hand, if you sell to a wholesaler, you might only make 94 percent of the market price, but you can count on receiving the agreed price immediately. "If you deal with a middleman, you can lock in the price," said Salem David of the Louisiana Gold and Silver Shop. "You send the gold by registered, insured mail, and they send you a check."

Refiners which purchase gold include the Ingelhard Minerals and Chemicals Corp. and Handy and Harman, both located in New York City. Wholesale gold dealers include J. Aron and Co., Inc., Mocatta Metals Corp., and Sharps Pixley, Inc., all of New York City. There are other, smaller dealers in major cities throughout the country.

Of course, your profit will depend on what you buy and how much you pay for it. That's where the testing equipment and good judgement comes in.

First of all, you have to establish whether the items presented to you for purchase are indeed gold. That's done with a scratch test. First, you cut the metal and then you apply nitric acid. It will not react if the item being tested is more than 40 percent gold, or about 10 karats. It will react if the gold content is less than that.

Another test is used to determine the purity of the gold, For this test, you apply a mixture of nitric and hydrochloric acids, known as an aqua regia solution. Depending on the amount of hydrochloric acid, the mixture will not react to gold above a certain degree of purity.

Of course, you can also rely on the karat mark inscribed in many gold pieces, if you trust it. But judging the purity of gold is an inexact science, especially when you buy from anyone who walks in the door. "There's no way to know absolutely, exactly," Said Leo Roit, owner of the General Gold Exchange in Los Angeles. "You have to be very careful."

Once you know the purity of the product you are buying, you can estimate how much you can resell it for through a formula that gives you a price per pennyweight. Naturally, you want to pay less for the item than you will make when you resell it. The question is, how much less?

Dealers say the margin ranges from 5 percent to 50 percent, but is generally around 20 percent. In most cases, it depends on subjective judgments. If you think the price will rise before you resell it, you can cut your margin. If you want to protect yourself from losses in case the price drops, you have to pay less.

Other factors enter into it, too. You can pay more if you are sure the product is pure and it isn't stolen. Competition also comes into play, since the public will be looking for the highest price it can get.

It doesn't really matter what type of gold you buy or how many karats it is, since you will set your price according to pure gold content. However, most dealers will not bother with gold plated or gold fill products, since the gold content is too low to make them worthwhile.

But no matter what product you buy, you must guard against an incorrect estimate of its purity. You could lose a lot of money if you overestimate the number of karats or mistake gold plated items for solid gold.

Some dealers develop a sideline to their scrap gold business by watching for high quality pieces of jewelry, which they can sell as jewelry, rather than scrap gold.

Those dealers who refine the scrap gold they buy before selling it say refining gives them an edge when it comes to reselling their gold. "It gives you an absolute edge, because you know exactly what it's worth and you get it," said Frank Kopesdy, owner of a Chicago gold shop.

You also have to turn your gold over as quickly as possible for two reasons. First, you don't make any money until you resell. Second, the quicker you sell, the less chance there is of loss or theft.

Most dealers ship their gold by registered, insured mail or through a courier service. You can also buy special insurance policies to cover your operation against loss or theft, but small-scale dealers say this is too expensive given their profit margin.

The biggest challenge to a gold dealer is to avoid buying fake or stolen merchandise. A dealer must also avoid misjudging the items he is buying or the price he is paying given the quality of the item and the price of gold.

"My advice to somebody starting out would be to keep adequate records and try to keep from getting involved in stolen merchandise," said David. "Use common sense," he said, like looking for a name or initials in rings to verify that the seller is in fact the owner.

So why go into the gold business? "It's easy," David said. And you can make a good living. As another Chicago dealer put it, "You have a good solid business that can go on indefinetly and the best part is, you don't have to work for anybody ever again."

GOLD JEWELERS SCALES:
RENT—LEASE—BUY

Robert Arnay Inc.
37 W. 47th Street
New York, NY

Itin Scale Company
431 Avenue U.
Brooklyn, NY

Electronic Digital Scales
2 Street E.
Rockaway, NY

CASH BUYERS OF GOLD, SILVER and PLATINUM:
TRADE ONLY

Goldhorn Refiners, Inc.
44 West 47th Street
New York, NY 10036

Northeastern Gold & Refining Co.
104 Canal Street
New York, NY

Ross Refiners
587 5th Avenue
New York, NY

(Some of these dealers also buy Diamonds!)

GOLD TESTING EQUIPMENT & JEWELERS SUPPLIES.
TRADE ONLY

A & M Jewelers Tool & Supplies
36 W 46th Street
New York, NY

William Dixon, Inc.
750 Washington Avenue
Crist, New Jersey

Caline Corporation
14 Main Street
Belleville, New Jersey

JEWELRY STORE DISPLAY ITEMS (Display Cases.)

Fixman Jewerlers Supply Co.
72 Bowery Street
New York, NY

Edwin Freed, Inc.
151 W 46 Street
New York, NY

Kassoy, Inc.
30 W. 47th Street
New York, NY

To check daily gold prices call a local stock broker or a gold wholesaler. It's best to check with both on a daily basis.

Gold, Silver & Platinum Dealers

A-1 AGES AGO ANTIQUES
"THE HIGHER BUYER"
Always Buying
Top Dollar Will Be
Paid For Silver, Gold,
Gold Filled Any Form
Paying Premium For: Silverware,
Tea Sets, Trays, Souvenir Spoons,
Jewelry, Watches, Coins
Also: Dental, Scrap Any Form
722-8700
1421 S Broadway —————————— 722-8700

ALL AMERICAN DIAMOND GOLD & SILVER EXCHANGE
BUYING & SELLING
2330 S Broadway —————————— 722-3222

American International Exchange Inc
13155 Wide Acres Rd ————————— 238-2109
Antique Jewelry Exchange 3905 S Broadway – 781-3462
Arapahoe Coins & Stamps 6552 S Broadway – 797-0466
AURORA GOLD & SILVER EXCHANGE
Buckingham Square Shopping Center ——— 695-6220
CERTIFIED INVESTMENT BROKERS
Investment Specialists
Rare Coins, Bullion, Gold & Silver
Brokerage Buying & Selling
777 29 Boulder ——————————— 494-4470
CHERRY CREEK RARE COIN GALLERY
See Our Ad At Coin Dealers, Supplies, Etc
125 Adams ————————————— 320-8591
Collectors Coin Exchange
Cinderella City ——————————— 761-0101
COLORADO COLLECTORS CENTER
Quote Line 1724 S Broadway —————— 733-4844
See Our Ad Under Coin Dealers, Supplies, Etc
South Broadway 1724 S Broadway ———— 778-0453

Lakewood Gold & Silver Exchange
9715 W Colfax Av ——————————— 233-8798
LOWE'S RARE COINS
See Our Ad Under Coin Dealers, Supplies, Etc
7101 W Colfax Av ——————————— 232-8999
Marshall's Gold And Silver Inc
18 S Broadway ———————————— 722-2515
MOLBERG'S JEWELERS – GEMOLOGISTS
University Hills Mall —————————— 757-8325
PANDORA'S JEWEL BOX
HIGHEST PRICES PAID FOR
GOLD, SILVER, COINS, COLLECTIBLES
2017 S University Blvd ————————— 777-6724
420 16 ——————————————— 534-1791

PEASANT PEDDLER 7867 W Jewell Av —— 988-9254
PRECIOUS METAL PROCESSING CO
2601 Larimer ———————————— 294-0103
ROYAL GOLD AND SILVER EXCHANGE
Cash Buyers For
Gold, Silver And Diamonds
Gold & Silver Bullion
3120 S Parker Rd ——————————— 696-0770

SECURITY SILVER & GOLD EXCHANGE INC
GOLD & SILVER
COINS & BARS
NO SALES TAX
3400 W State Boise Id
Toll Free Dial 1 & Then ——————— 800 635-5353

Silver Cycle Ltd 6635 E Jamison Av ———— 771-4620
SOUTHGLENN GOLD & SILVER COIN EXCHANGE
Southglenn Mall ——————————— 797-3420
Stan's Colorado Gold & Coin Exchange
412 E Colfax Av ——————————— 837-8437
STRATEGIC METALS INTERNATIONAL INC
11728 Hwy 93 Boulder ————————— 499-1010
TEBO COIN CO OF BOULDER
2863 28 Boulder ——————————— 444-2646

CHAPTER FOUR

WHOLESALING YOUR WAY TO $72,000 A YEAR!

    Establishing your own wholesale women's clothing and accessory business is one of the easiest and least expensive ways to start yourself on the path to riches. Your initial expense can be as little as $30 and you can begin on a part-time basis, working only a few hours on the weekend. Best of all, from your very first day, you'll be reaping the rewards of your efforts. Amazingly you can collect a 100 percent profit or more on your very first sale and every sale thereafter.
    One of the main advantages of starting your wholesale business on a small scale is that you can make your business headquarters in your home. This eliminates the costly overhead of a separate facility and its furnishings. A small corner in your home or apartment is all the room you'll need in the beginning stages of your business. Later, as you grow, you can move your business area to an extra room in your home, the garage, or into your basement. Even in twelve months or less, when your income reaches $50,000 to $70,000 per year, a women's clothing wholesaler can still operate his business out of his home, keeping overhead at a minimum and profits at a maximum.

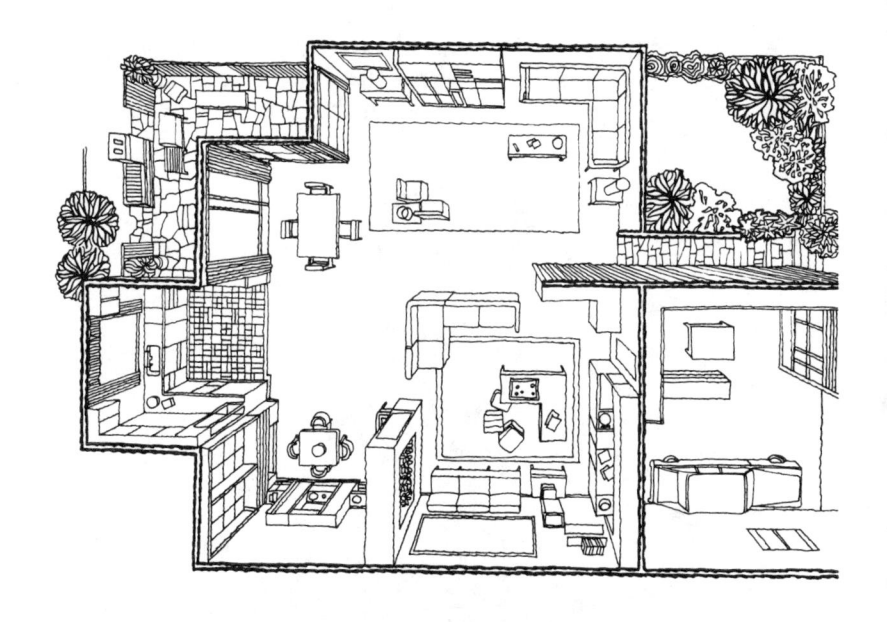

The place to start is the newspaper classified ads. *The New York Times* prints a section titled "Offerings To Buyers" each Sunday. Pick up a copy at your local (out-of-town newspapers) newsstand and read it carefully. You'll find a vast array of women's merchandise, such as sundresses, skirts, shoes, watches, jewelry and winter clothing. For the most part, these are manufacturer's samples, overruns and closeouts. The merchandise is usually first quality. Most important, the manufacturers are only one step away from giving this merchandise away.

You can expect to find offerings such as the following:
★ (Up to 80 per cent BELOW wholesale)
  Sundresses, $1.85 each
  100 pair earrings, $10.00
  Designer jeans, $5.00 pair
  Handbags: Straw, $1.00; Canvas, $1.00
  Name brand sweaters, $4.75 each
  Wrap-around skirts, $1.50 each
  T-shirts, $6.00 per dozen
  Pantyhose, $2.00 dozen
  Knit hats, 40 cents each
  Leather belts, $3.00 per dozen

Later, when your business has expanded, if you choose you can get into higher priced designer dresses, jackets, coats and more elaborate accessories offered at these same unbelievable prices.

Most of these manufacturers and distributors list their telephone numbers, many with toll-free 800 exchanges, and are happy to give you more information regarding their merchandise. Many also have catalogs and printed sheets listing their complete line of merchandise, descriptions and prices. A few will even send you a free sample of their merchandise. Call them and find out exactly what they have to offer. Be up front. Tell them you're starting your own wholesale business. They're business people, too, and most of them will do everything they can to help a potential customer get started.

All of these distributors operate on volume pricing. The more you buy, the cheaper your price per unit.

For the new entrepreneur who's placing his first order, they will allow their minimum pricing on any quantity as a first and only-time courtesy. Do take advantage of this opportunity with all your first orders. The usual procedure will be for your merchandise to be shipped COD by United Parcel.

One word of caution. Not all distributors are honest and instead of first quality merchandise you may receive cheap quality and irregulars. Since you're just beginning and don't have the funds to travel to the distributors' to examine the merchandise you'll be purchasing, buying in small quantities in the beginning will enable you to separate the honest distributors from the dishonest ones. Always make it clear to the distributor when you place your order that you expect quality merchandise and if you do not receive it, you will not purchase from him again.

Now that you know where and how to get your merchandise, how do you sell it and become a successful wholesaler? Let's choose one of the opportunity wholesalers' most popular items and see how it makes its way into the hands of the retailer.

Multi-printed, wrap-around skirts from Pakistan are offered by a number of reliable distributors at a minimum of $1.50 each. They're popular wherever they're sold, one size fits all, and women love to wear them year 'round. Because of their popularity, these distributors will definitely send you a sample if you explain that you'll be going into business and will be ordering more from them. You'll find that quality and selection are about equal, but usually one particular distributor's sample will catch your eye. Order 20 skirts for $30.00 from this distributor.

Your skirts will arrive in only a few days. Now check your local newspapers and area bulletin boards for flea markets being held in your locale during the next weekend. Make a list of these markets, according to their location, beginning with the closest to your home and ending with the one farthest away. Early on that first Saturday morning head for the first flea market on your list.

When you arrive, check out the stalls and the merchandise being offered for sale. Look for a stall that is low on merchandise or is offering merchandise that doesn't fall into the most popular category. Now show your samples and go into your best sales pitch. Emphasize the popularity of the skirts and their high profit margin. Explain that even in stores you rarely see these skirts *on sale* for less than $12.00. Then offer your 20 skirts to him for $3.00 each. Assure him that he can price them at $7, $8, or even $10. That's a super profit potential for him and very hard to turn down.

As for you, don't be surprised if you sell your skirts at the first flea market on your list and in a very short period of time. That amounts to $60.00 per hour for you! And, of course, the more skirts you purchase initially, the more per hour you'll be earning.

Now take your first $60.00 earnings and place another "first" order with another distributor for 40 skirts at $1.50 each. Call your first customer. His previous success will make him eager to purchase all 40 of these skirts at $120. If he can't take all 40, then go to the next flea market on your list. Again, don't be surprised if you've now made $120 for one hour's work.

Continue this procedure, honing your sales skills and collecting names and telephone numbers of your flea market customers. And be sure you always leave your name and telephone number with the vendor. He won't hesitate to call you when he wishes to reorder. In time you'll want to have your own business cards printed with your name, telephone number and title of wholesaler. When you hand them out it's always a good idea to jot down on the back the merchandise the vendor ordered or has shown an interest in.

Keep a record book of all your clients, their names, addresses, telephone numbers, the type of merchandise they purchased, the amount of the sale and their check number.

This is not only for the Internal Revenue Service. Later you'll save time calling your clients rather than visiting the flea markets over and over again. Then you can concentrate on visiting markets further down on your list and on the new ones opening in your area.

Don't limit your sales efforts only to flea markets. Check the Yellow Pages of your telephone book, study newspaper ads carefully and make a list of all the discount women's clothing stores in your area. Again, begin with the one closest to your home and end with the one farthest away. Avoid discount chain stores. Their buying is usually done at a central location and your local store managers do not have the authority to purchase from you, no matter how good the deal.

Visit all the independent stores on your list. Again, don't be surprised how quickly your skirts will sell to discount women's clothing stores, especially those located in discount clothing malls. Add these new customers and all the relevant information to your record book. You'll also want to be telephoning them again.

You don't have to limit yourself to women's discount clothing stores. It's worth your time to check out independent variety and novelty stores and drug stores. Never underestimate the sales potential of your product and the attractiveness of the incredible freedom of markup allowed the purchaser.

You can also sell your product to schools and charities which are involved in fundraising. Always check out city and town celebration days where there will be money-raising booths. Call area Chamber of Commerce offices for this information. Fairs and traveling carnivals are also often in need of fresh merchandise to sell in their gift booths. Just show up at these affairs and show the booth manager your best salesmanship and your merchandise.

Uncover Your True Potential...

It's amazing how quickly you'll find yourself selling as many as 500 skirts per week, most of them repeat orders which are called into your home. Of course, you'll now be purchasing in volume and getting the lowest possible price as a matter of course. Your 1000 $1.50-each skirts will cost you $1,500 but you'll be selling them for $3,000. With your incredibly low overhead, that's about $1,500 per week profit. That's $6,000 per month, based on four weeks per month, and a whopping $72,000 per year for a part-time effort you can do on the weekend!

As your customers and profits increase, you can expand your inventory. Add other items of women's apparel and accessories. The more profit-making items you offer your customers, the more they'll buy and the higher the profits. In turn, they'll have more money for future purchases from you.

You might also consider producing a bi-monthly mailing to all your customers. List your newest products and prices and remind them of your most popular and highest profit-making items. This newsletter or flyer can be a simple 8½ by 11 sheet, typed on one side, copied, and folded over and stapled with the customer's name and address on the outside. Cost: less than $45 per mailng including postage. It's simple to do and will serve several purposes. It will keep your customers up-to-date on the newest money-making items you can offer to them. It will remind the customer of you and stimulate him to immediately place an order he may have been putting off. And it's an excellent advertisement and inducement to buy when you send it to potential customers.

The day will probably come when you'll choose to go full-time as a wholesaler. Should you choose to personally visit neighboring states and extend your mailings even further from your home base, your gross income could rise to $140,000 or more per year. And you'll still be maintaining a minimum overhead by working out of your home and achieving maximum profit.

There's definitely big money in wholesaling out of your home. How much of it ends up in your pocket depends on you. And you don't have to wait to get started. This week could put you on the road to making the kind of money you only dreamed of before.

> "I don't mind being a company man as long as I own the company."

HANDBAGS

Over 300 Styles All One Price

$2.25 EACH

Large canvas, fashion vinyl, quilted nylon etc. All current. Retail to $12. All guaranteed. And you have a full exchange privilege for any bags you do not sell. Mail orders accepted via telephone, or stop by our showroom.
Our 9th Yr Advertising in the Times

G&G HANDBAGS
310 Fifth Ave., NY, NY 10001
212-736-0542

SUMMER CLOSEOUT
DIRECT FROM MFR

We have started to close-out many of our summer items, (from 20-50%) to make room for our fall and winter line. T-Shirts and blouses start $24 dz
Jogging suits at $7 each
Swishrt crop tops at $33 dz
Cut-off swtshirts at $57 dz
Summer skirts at $34 dz
Summer dresses at $7 each
Many other items are available at equally low prices. All are guaranteed first quality and are perfect for ssmll stores, home sales, flea markets and fund raisers. For more information contact:
R & R Gaver 212-858-2143
267 Douglass St., Bklyn, N.Y. 11217

ATTN: FLEA MKT VENDORS,
FUND RAISERS & PEDDLERS

We are first when it comes to new HOT items. Come to one source for back-to-school supplies toys, bisque, stickers, pens, tube socks, balloons, baseball cards, water guns, pinwheels, bubbles, pocket knives, kites, visors, beach balls, purses, combs, key chains, pins, perfume, wallets, etc. New items arrive daily. We have one of the largest selections of merchandise. Over 1500 different items. All merchandise on display. Send for free catalogue or visit our showroom.

MILLS SALES CO.
889 Bway, Crnr 19 St, NY, NY 10003
212-477-1000

SMI MFG INC.
Buy Direct from Manufacturer
576 3 Ave, Cor 15 St, Bklyn NY 11215

768-7666 OR 800-232-0200

Children's tube socks $2.75/dz
Boy's tube socks $3.75/dz
Ladies' Pastel Tube Socks $4.75/dz
Men's Briefs $7.20/dz
Boy's Briefs $6/dz
Ladies' Panties $7.20/dz
Girl's Panties $6/dz
All briefs and panties avail in 100% cotton or nylon.
Ladies' Opaque Sheer Panty Hose, Assorted Colors $7.20/dz
Ladies' Opaque Knee-Hi's
Assorted Colors $5.00/dz
WHOLESALE ONLY
FREE PARKING

CLOSE OUT LIST-
TO QUALIFIED BUYERS

HUNDREDS OF CLOSEOUTS, SPECIAL PURCHASES, ETC. AVAIL. TO YOU ON A REGULAR BASIS. IF YOU ARE A QUALIFIED BUYER, SEND DETAILS ON YOUR LETTERHEAD, OR ENCLOSE BUSINESS CARD FOR LISTING.

-GREENFIELD INDUSTRIES-
21 COTTERS LANE
E. BRUNSWICK NJ 08816
201-238-2112

BIG SPECIALS ON THE
FOLLOWING ELECTRONICS

Sanyo Model FT-222 $55
Model FT-3 Car Stereo 22
Model 693 3-way Speaker 13
Model 694 4-way Speaker 13
Model 695 5-way Speaker 14
Model GX78 3-way Box Speaker 17
Model GX58 3-way Mini Box Spkr 11
Model 702 7-Band Equalizer 17
Model 207 7-Band Equalizer 16
Cordless Telephone 55
Hand/Held Telephone 8
Ref. 12" B&W TV 48
Ref. 19" Color TV 180
Ref. 19" Color Remote TV 225

To place an order, or for info call:
212-387-1157
GRANADA ELECTRONICS INC.
485 Kent Ave, Bklyn NY 11211
11211

PHONES
& ACCESSORIES
-WHOLESALE-
-LOWEST PRICES In Town-
...Long Coil Cords $2.80 Ea.
...Trendline TT phones-orange, blue/red, green $38.95 Ea in Lots.
...Phones by Paul Nelson

BABY BELL, INC.
126 W, 26 St, NYC 10001
(212) 255-8888

T-SHIRTS

Sweat Shirts-Sweat Pants
and Fashion Sportswear
Childrens, Womens, Mens Sizes

To Jobbers, Flea Marketeers
and Promo Users

-LOW, LOW PRICES
-LOW MIN. ORDERS ACCEPTED
-CUSTOM IMPRINTING

PLYMOUTH MILLS INC.
212-447-6707   212-594-0120

T-SHIRTS, SWEAT SHIRTS, MUSCLE SHIRTS, IN STOCK

MEN'S AND BOY'S CAMO T-SHIRTS

CALL US TOLL FREE 1-800-321-0139.
SEE US IN LAS VEGAS! HILTON HOTEL BOOTHS 1013-1015 AUGUST 28-SEPT 1 1983.
BAY RAG 1210 STERLING RD, BAY 7B, DANIA FLA 33004 305-921-6865/305-949-6399.

6x9 Car Speakers

3 way $15
4 way $16
5 way $17

Car Stereo AM/FM Cassette $24
Pyramid 7 Band Equilizer $20
10 Band equilizer $24
700' Cordless phone $55
Car Stereo AM/FM Cas Auto/Rev .. $38
BROADWAY DISTR.   (516)294-2754

NAME BRAND ELECTRONICS WHOLESALER

Sony, Toshiba, Aiwa, Panasonic
Wholesale Box Lot Only
UNIGLOBE INTERNATL INC
111 W 30 St, NY 10001
(212)563-7340

Seiko $20

Seiko men's Q D/D Stainless $32
Seiko men's Q, leather band, gold . $55
Seiko ladie's Q leather band, gold $40
Casio Watches .... FROM $5.50
Orient Watches Auto 21J $23

VENUS TIME   (212)947-5352

HANDBAGS & KNAPSACKS
Canvas or Nylon

Dir from mfr. $2/ea & up. Lg. sel.
Ample parking.   Vola Bag Company
129 26th Street   Brooklyn   788-0993

100,000 PCS
LADIES IRREG Nightgowns

Asstd styles & sizes at $1 ea. Priced to sell. Thomas Antoniello Textiles, 351 Broadway NYC. 212-925-1152

TURQUOISE

Better quality chip inlay/sterling. Full line of proven winners. Free catalog.
(201)780-0478

T-SHIRTS/JERSEYS

CHILD's, MEN'S, LADIES
VARIETY: White, Black, Pastls
LOW PRICES   212-889-6210.

T-SHIRTS/JERSEYS

CHILD's, MEN'S, LADIES
VARIETY: White, Black, Pastls
LOW PRICES   212-889-6210.

ATTENTION VENDORS

Ladies & kids jogging suits, tall tops & sweaters 212-868-0269 or 516-242-5330

SCRUB SUITS & LAB COATS

Lab jackets, pants and baker's coats.
Direct from factory. (212)768-1622.

SALE ON ADULT VIDEO

Full feature, 70 titles, all orig & new. $18.25/ea. Quantity only 313/881-2927

COTTON TUBE SOCKS
Emby-7 W 30 St, NYC   594-5740

VIDEO TAPE-T120-$5.50/6.50
TDK-TYP-HG-VHS. COD. 212-996-5130

TOYS NOVELTIES & WATCHES

Rollover Buggies...$2.10 ea.; Laughing Clown, Musical Santa Claus, Sonic Dogs, Bic Lighters($4.00 Dz), Kiddie Stickers($3.00 Dz.50 Styles), Velcro Wallets(50 Styles), Disco Bags(1d Colors), Hat Packs(100 Styles,$2.50 Dz)
CATALOG   STAR TRACK
Send $3(Refundable)   516-598-1529
182A Park Ave Amityville, NY 11701

COTTON SWEATERS

Crewneck, 13 colors $8.50. Striped $13.50. Heavy knit $13.50. XS-XL.

CHECKED COOK SHIRTS

Pocket, button front. Red/black, gray/black, Fuchsia/blk $6.50 S-M-L.

Overdyed Chemical-Warfare Pants.
One size fits all. 9 colors $6.50
Free brochure. Call Suzy 212-226-1130

FALL FASHIONS FAMOUS LABEL

JEANS, JACKETS,
ACTIVE WEAR
212-232-2273/259-7600/232-2051
U.P.S/C.O.D.

ATTENTION: MICROWAVE ANTENNA DEALERS

Star I $40 (LR3); Star 2 $42, MDC 43/23 $75, MDC 23b $55. All in lots of 10. Other Video accessories available Prompt courteous service. Free delivery. Fair over the counter exchange. 212-780-0167

WATCHES

Full selection of LCD, quartz & mech'ls. Chicklets-12colors, lowest price & best quality. Flea mktrs & peddlers invited. Min $200. Bella Watch 37 W39 St 11flr, NYC. 212-730-1137

TELEPHONES

TOP QUALITY REMANUFACTURED, BOXED, READY FOR SALE.

Pay stations, 2500, 2200, 80E.
Low prices. Call Mr. Lee 617-676-4526

Ladies Neckwear

Cummerbunds, bow ties, ties, sashes, silks. At Once Delivery 212-686-9786.

SERGIO VALENTE MENS BRIEFS

100%   Cotton.Sizes   S,M,L,XL
Min order 24 doz. $13.50/doz Qty orders of 100 doz or more $12/doz
Mr. Neil (212)253-3133

Folding Sunglasses .... $17.95 dz
Lined Rubber Gloves .... $3.96 dz
Disposbl Gas Lighters ...... $2.75 dz
98c Toothbrushes .... 12c ea
DM SALES   911 Bway   212-254-8320

HANDBAGS-Straw handbags 1.00 each; Canvas handbags $1.00 & Up; Vinyl bags made in USA $2 each
TRAVEL BAGS-90% OFF RETAIL.
UPS/COD. Call F.I.E. 212-834-1715

ATTENTION: JOBBERS-LIQUIDATORS-Bankruptcies-Etc-If you have a lg quantity of any item-& it's priced right-we have a client list of 2200 wholesalers 201/628-0434-Ask for Ron

CHILDREN'S CLOTHING

new born thru size 7, below wholesale.
Ms Asher 914-739-7653.

SHEET SETS & nightgowns, very low price. Craft co., 50 Bond St. NY, NY 10012 or call 777-6916 ask for Sol.

14K/SS Direct Source Full Line Chains Charms, earr, closeouts/kits. Chritam Intl Mfg/Imp 212-278-2418 UPS/COD

ATT: WAGON JOBBERS
WHOLESALERS-RETAILERS
FLEA MARKETS-ETC

BIG DISCOUNTS ON
SCHOOL SUPPLIES

SUNGLASSES, GIFTS, CAMERAS, FILMS, BATTERIES, LIGHTERS, PENS, LITE BULBS, STATY, PADLOCKS, CLOCKS, UMBRELLAS, ELECTRIC SHAVERS, HAIRDRYERS, SCOTCH TAPE, FLASH LITES, TOOL KITS, KEYCHAINS, SHOE LACES, BALOONS, ETC

ALL BRANDS&ALL MAKES
If You're Looking For Price Call Us
If You're Looking for long credit terms DON'T call us.

PRICE KING INC
677-1270 890 Bway NY 10001
Corner 19th St Open Sunday 11-5PM

CHICKLETS $1.70

RIBBON CHICKLETS $1.80
MEN'S CHICKLETS $1.90
MECHANICAL WATCHES $4
CALCULATORS $2.60
TWISTO FLEX $2.20

LADIES DIVERS WATCHES	$1.90
MEN'S DIVERS WATCHES	$2.10
MEN'S CHICKLETS gold	$2.50
MEN'S CHICKLETS chrome	$2.50
5/F LCD	$1.45
QUARTZ ANALOGUE	$10.00
VERTICAL WATCHES	$2.10
FANCY LIGHTER WATCHES	$6.25
PEN WATCH BLACK/GOLD	$1.90
LCD MESH BAND	$1.95
KIDDIES PVC Band Watches	$1.60
CALCULATOR MELODY	$3.95
CALCULATOR Gold Tone	$3.25
CALCULATOR Marble	$3.75

Large quantities only UPS/COD
SONEX EXPORT LTD
295 Fifth Avenue Rm 502 (Bet 30-31St)
CALL MIKE 212-532-1255/56

FOLDING SUNGLASSES

$16.00/DOZEN

5/F LCD........$1.50
PEN WATCH...$1.40
TELEPHONES..$7.00
CHICKLET.....$1.70

ONLY LARGE QUANTITIES

212-695-3830

CORRUGATED BOXES

JOB LOTS

4 x 4 x 4 no ptg.	7c
7¼ x 2 x 9½ no ptg.	10c
8 x 5 x 17 ptd	13c
9¾ x 4 x 13 no ptg.	10c
9¼ x 9¼ x 16½ ptd. (275 T)	30c
10 x 6 x 8 ptd.	17c
11½ x 7½ x 10 ptd	15c
11¼ x 8¾ x 9 ptd (275 T)	25c
11 x 6½ x 7 ptd.	14c
12⅞ x 4⅜ x 8¼ ptd	12c
13 x 13 x 14 ptd.	29c
13 x 9 x 5 ptd.	15c
13½ x 7½ x 5½ ptd.	15c
14 x 6 x 7 ptg	12c
15¾ x 8 x 6 ptd.	15c
16 x 11 x 4 ptd.	16c
16⅞ x 6⅜ x 22 ptd. (275 T)	33c
16½ x 6 x 10 ptd.	15c
22 x 15 x 22 ptd	57c
28 x 21 x 41 ptd (350 T D/W) (used)	59c
37¼ x 22½ x 16 no ptg (350 T D/W) (used)	55c

WINSTON BOX CO.
575 Gotham Parkway
Carlstadt, N.J. 07072
201-933-7500 212-244-0345
Minimum order $135 on above prices.

FOLDING SUNGLASSES

$16.50/DOZEN

5/F LCD........$1.50
PEN WATCH...$1.40
TELEPHONES..$8.00
CHICKLET.....$1.70

ONLY LARGE QUANTITIES

212-695-3830

TELEPHONES

10 MEMORIES
W/music on hold, wall bracket, ringer on/off, last # redial.

$14.00 EACH

PHONE
RADIO AM/FM
ALARM CLOCK
(ALL IN ONE)
$24.00 EACH

Large Quantities Only UPS/COD
SONEX EXPORT LTD.
295 Fifth Avenue Rm 502 (bet 30-31st)
CALL MIKE 212-532-1255

WALKMAN CASSETTE UNISEF BRAND

(MADE IN JAPAN)

MODEL V-1 $10.75
Stereo Cass. Player

MODEL V-7 $19.00
Stereo Cass. AM/FM Radio

MODEL AF 1100 $25.50
Stereo Cass. Recorder AM/FM Radio W/Built in Speaker

MODEL AF 1200 $29.50
Stereo Cass. Recorder Player AM/FM Radio W/Built in Speaker & Auto shut off.

MODEL AF2000 $29.50
AM/FM Stereo detachable Cass. Recorder w/built in speakers.

All above models with head phones.
Several different models also avail.
Large quantatiies only UPS/COD
SONEX EXPORT LTD.
295 Fifth Avenue Rm 502 (Bet 30-31St)
CALL MIKE 212-532-1255/56

XMAS IN THE SUMMER
CLOSEOUT

Over 150 items at 25 to 50% below regular factory prices. Paper, Bows, Ribbons, Tags, Cards, Garlands, Boxes, etc. Earn an extra 10% off closeout prices now thru Sept. 2

EXAMPLES:

16 Shts Flat Paks	75C net
100 S.F. Jumbo log paper	$1.67 net
20 Ct. Bow Bag	38C net
20 Ct. Solid Cards boxed	$1.02 net

Many many others come in and see us or call.

HILMOR SALES CO.
7777 Westside Ave.
No. Bergen, N.J. 201-662-1900

-CLOSE OUT LIST-
TO QUALIFIED BUYERS

HUNDREDS OF CLOSEOUTS, SPECIAL PURCHASES, ETC. AVAIL. TO YOU ON A REGULAR BASIS. IF YOU ARE A QUALIFIED BUYER, SEND DETAILS ON YOUR LETTERHEAD, OR ENCLOSE BUSINESS CARD FOR LISTING.

-GREENFIELD INDUSTRIES-
21 COTTERS LANE
E.BRUNSWICK NJ 08816
201-238-2112

MEN'S JEANS $60DZ

Men's L.S..Western $48dz
Men's Cham Lk Dr Shirt $66dz
Color Cotton Briefs $9dz
BVD Men's Tee's, irr $13.50dz
Hanes Boy's Tee's, irr $8dz
Men's Designer look jkts ..... $8.50 ea
Fancy cotton polos .... $27 dz
FREE CATOLOGUE-YOUNG'S
319 Grand St. NYC, 10002 212-226-4333.

T-SHIRTS

LONG & SHORT SLEEVE
SWEATSHIRTS FROM CHINA

HEALTH-LOOM CORP
40 West 17 St, NYC (212) 989-8600

DISCO SUNGLASSES
w/blinking light
Bi-Trifold Velcro Wallets
Duffle Bag Key Chain Light Up Rose
Spin Robot, Puffy Stickers & novelties
LEADING CREATIONS INC
1225 Bway Rm803, NY 212-686-4200

FRAGRANCES & COSMETICS
Nationally Advertised Brands
LOWEST WHOLESALE PRICES
Specializing in Exports
ROSS COSMETICS 212-273-4144
135 Canal St, Staten Isl, NY 10304
Mon to Fri 9-5   Sat by appt only

LARGE SIZES
Ladies lg & missy blouses,skrts,
MUSCLE SHIRTS, sweats & jogging
sets.Large Size Center 520 Bway
966-6424

5000+ items. Stationery, toys, pens,
etc. Stickers, $3.75/dz; Sticker books,
$6/dz; Racquet balls, .65c/can; .79c
5x8 book, .20c/ea.. Closeouts, showroom. Cs lots. Cat avail 516-420-1911
A&H 226 Rt 109 Farmingdale NY 11735

Folding knives, $11.99 Dozen.
1st quality, about ½" when opened.
1-800-231-3144/212-696-5618/9742

P.B.S. JEWELRY
Colored earrings $3.75 doz
548-58th St, Bklyn. 492-2402 eves

MERCHANDISE OFFERED
Bev Styles. Closeouts on skirts, shirts,
jeans, & blouses. 212-594-7125.

BUY DIRECTLY from Mfgrs womens
& childrens active wear. Ideal for jobbers, flea mkts & store openings. All
colors, close out prices. Call Holly
mornings or Eves 516-785-5288

CHICKLETS $1.70. Twistoflex $2.20.
Lge selection of quartz analogue from
$11 & up. Walkman AM/FM radio
$8.50. Lg quantities. Only UPS/COD.
Call Tom, 212-684-6290/98

SWEATERS, Blouses, Corduroy pants,
skiwear, active wear. Prices can't be
beat. We ship sample packages, UPS
COD anywhere in the USA. 212-
695-8099 Gabys Juniors.

MFR HAS FLEECE & VELOUR
JOGGING SUITS.
CALL (201) 388-1919

NEW FALL SWEATERS, BLOUSES,
SKIRTS, CORDUROY PANTS.
Wholesale.   Call 516-872-8560

T-SHIRTS & Baseball JERSEYS. Direct from importer. Superior qual.
212-243-2176 11-7pm   Open 7 days.

Pantyhose $2/dz; Famous holiday gift
wrap $26/dz; Giant value Christmas
cards (30) $35/dz; Octopus or Spider
wall walker $.90/dz; Balloon Asst
(100) $11.40/case; Confetti (50 bags)
$2/case; Deluxe metal noisemakers
(50) $26.80/case. Min order $20.
Check/money order:
Carla Lamberson 390 Clocks Blvd,
E. Massapequa NY 11758 516-798-4054
9-4PM Mon—Fri Only.....NO COD

JEWELRY
CLOSE OUTS

GENUINE TURQUOISE
Ring & pendants .... $3.60 Dozen
Earrings .... $5.00 Dozen
Lighter cases .... $12 Dozen
100,000 items, non-tarnish, $25
Sample COD. Color Cat 800-392-2532

INTERLOCK
L/S JOGGERS
$72/DOZEN
201-431-0880

CHEAP-CHEAP
SCHOOL OPENING SPECIAL
$1.79 Spiral Bks,3sub $6.60dz
$2.49 Hardcover Books $13.20dz
$3.50 64 Crayons $13.20dz
$1.79 12pc Marker Set $6.00dz
OPEN 7 DAYS   (212)875-8760

TOOL CLOSEOUT
Thirty 4" vices $13. Thirty 5" vices
$15. Thirty 6" vices $20. Ten 2-ton
floor jacks $85. Six 4-ton port-a-power
kits $77. Twenty-five 4 pc. gear polar
sets $25. Ten 6" wood joiners (elec-
tric) $185. All or part. 516-466-4598

Att: Jobbers, Flea Marketeers, Hus-
tlers. Closing out brand name applian-
ces, S.S pots, open stock dinnerware,
luggage, tote bags, clocks, watches &
other housewares. Huge quantities, all
below distributor cost. Gross, 436-5509

Frag & Cosm-Brand Names
Closeout prices. (516)328-6688
Arlene Weinman & Assoc. Inc

FAMOUS LABEL JOG SUITS
At way below wholesale. From $11.75
Asrted jacq & pointel sweaters, $4.75.
UPS COD. 201/641-6260

PHONES $7.25
10 Memory $13.00
Large Quantity Only (212)924-5191

CHILDRENS CLOTHES
Complete Line-Low Prices, designer
jeans, also Jr/Misses (201)530-8750

T-SHIRTS $7/dz
BASEBALL JERSEY $11/dz
212-725-2027

Fashion Belts-Assorted $3 dz.
Extra overrun, min 6 dz. Perry's,
873 B'Way, NY,NY 10003.212-475-9100

L&M TRADING
Wholesalers of perfume & colognes
212-634-3944

CHILDREN'S WEAR
BRAND NAMES-LOW PRICES
212-941-8221

POLY Pull-On Pants, Poly Pull-On
Pleated Skirts. Missy & X-Lge sizes.
Mfr...212-391-6663

TAPEX CLOCK RADIO AM/FM w/BUILT-IN PHONE ... $26.75

One piece phones w/mem $7.50
Credit Card Calculators $3.00
1600 watt Hair Blowers $5.00
Toasters or Irons $8.50
50 pc Stainless Steel Flatware ... $8.00
Tapex Stain Steel Dlx Cookware $12.00
Quartz Heaters $12.75
Tapex Indoor Antennas $16.00
Tapex Outdoor Antennas $24.00
Osc Fans 12" & 16" In Stock
SAJRA DISTRIBUTORS
150 W 28th St, NYC 10001
(212) 620-0707

WISHNIK TROLLS
ARE BACK! 3½" hi-in own container. Each outfitted (i.e. Love-nik, Lucky-nik) 12 Asst styles, Pkd 3/d/counter dsply $18/dz min 3 dz. WISH-NIK Pufty Stickers, $6/dz min 3 dz. Giant 27" x 39" clr poster, $24/dz min 2 dz. Send check now, & we pay the shipping.
JAMCOR LICENSING CORP.
5 Winmere Plc. or call 516-586-2275

FLYING BIRD

RUBBERBAND W/U

$1.25/PC

MIN.QTY 12 DZ

212-786-6253

SEIKO WATCH $16
FULL LINE OF SEIKO WATCHES
FERRARI WATCH $1.75
CORDLESS PHONE 700' $55
WORLDTIME 1225 Bway 212-725-0233

7,000 Pairs womens fall casual shoes. 500 Dozen white spay paints. Also housewares, toys, wearing apparel, hardware, etc. Lg & small lots. Gd for flea markets & discount stores. Joro Sales Co., 300 W. Elizabeth Ave, Linden, N.J., 201-862-5654.

FOLDING Sunglasses $15.50
DIAMOND CUT $15.50
AM/FM STEREO $8.50
1225 Bway, Rm 307, NYC 212-689-5495

5,000
UNIFORMS & HOUSE SMOCKS
Ass't Colors & Sizes, Reg. $36/Doz. Closeout $15/Doz.Min 10 doz.ass't. Will ship COD,UPS, Mr.A, 592-3100

Semi-Precious Bead Necklaces
Amethyst, malachite, onyx, sodalite, jade, tiger eye, rosequartz, carnelian, etc. Low, low prices.
Transworld 565 5th Ave OX 7-8770

DESIGNER JEANS
Jordache $21-SergioValente $20.75
Gloria Vndblt $18.50-Calvin $18.50
Gloria Vndblt Crayons $16-Lee $12.75
All Brands UPS/COD 212-253-8010

DRESSES, SUITS, SPRTSWR
Mfr's closeout/below wholesale
E Simon, 254 W 35 St, NYC, 868-5636

PIERCED EARRINGS
$36 a Gross, assorted colors, for COD delivery. 516-475-8675

HOTTEST ITEMS!
Satin ties, bandanas, painters caps, shirts. 201-568-7626 or 201-364-8317

STYLISH CLOSEOUT DRESSES
$6 and up. Transitional & Fall
UPS/COD   (201)678-5144

WHOLESALE
APPAREL
NEW JERSEY'S FASTEST
GROWING DISTRIBUTOR
Jobbers, Merchants, Other Agents:

SPECIAL
y-neck sweaters, $60 per doz
jr. & missy sportswear, pants, skirts, & tops, large selection.
HUDSON WHOLESALE
327 HUDSON ST.
HACKENSACK, NJ
201-489-7282   Jack/Tony

DOWN SKI VESTS
Childrens sizes, S, M, L, XL (6-20), $7/per vest for vol buyer.
MISC OUTLET LIQUIDATORS
215-295-1759

EELSKIN
HANDBAGS & ACCESSORIES
COMBINATION EEL/LEATHER
VARIOUS STYLES & COLORS
TOP QUALITY & PRICES
OCEAN IMPORTS INC
347 5th Ave Ste 1005 NY, NY 10016
212-725-0777

FERRARI SUNGLASSES
$16/dz

Chickets $1.65
Only large quantities
(212)685-2850   UPS/COD
DISCOUNT BUYING SERVICE reports/researches/buys/samples, jeans, etc.,under $5. Special attention new stores/minorities

HOWARD KAPLAN
212-868-9337/1-800-431-1953(24hrs)

GIVEAWAY DEAL
From Paris, France, barrettes, combs, bob-pins, hairpins where $18-$48 dozen
GIVEAWAY PRICE $1.00 DOZEN
516-799-2346 or 516-795-6204 UPS

COSTUME JEWELRY
Assorted boxed pendant necklaces $9.00 per dz, retail value over $10.00 per piece, money back guarantee.
Call 412-367-4406 anytime

PERFUME & COLOGNES
ALL NAME BRANDS, UP TO 60% DISCOUNT, 1225 BROADWAY,
RM 412, NYC, 10001 212-889-8681

BRAND NAME
PERFUMES & COLOGNES
212-989-8765. 11 W. 25 ST, NYC 10010

CLOSE OUT/
SUMMER MERCHANDISE
695-3606 Monday-Friday 9-6

NECKTIES, BOW TIES
500 DZ Silk's, Polyester's. Much Below Mfgr Cost. Also...Closeouts 212-684-3296.

BLOUSES   SWEATERS   SKIRTS
PANTS at LOW LOW PRICES. JAS
FASHION 85 Allen St. 212-925-1031

SHEET SETS-BELOW wholesale-current name brands-all colors & sizes, many patterns, low min. 212-361-7400

DUMP
T-SHIRTS & BASEBALL JERSEYS
ALSO CUSTOM SCREEN PRINTING
LOW RATES   (212) 564-7150

KNIFE special 3" $7.20 dz. 4" $9 dz. 5" $13 dz. 6" $21/dz. 6½" $27 dz. 212-725-2027

GOOD ITEMS for premium companies, jobbers, flea markets & exporters Write-Box 211, Island Park, NY 11558

NAME BRAND Infants, Childrens to Sz 14, Jr Clothes. 50% Below Wholesale! 212-594-6038/1-800-223-7780

LADIES SPORTSWEAR
FLEA MKTS & VENDORS
FAMOUS LABELS
UP TO 70% OFF
CALL CLAIRE 516-239-4466
BEN ELIAS INDUSTRIES

ACTIVE SPORTSWEAR
MFR CLOSING OUT
SUMMER STOCK OF WOMENS
1ST QUALITY FULL CUT GARMENTS
UPS/COD/2 DOZEN MINIMUM
T.C.& CO (201) 388-1919
15 Walnut Ave, Clark, NJ 07066

SEICO WATCHES
Seico from $19.95
Citizen from $17.94
Orient from $19.95
Casio from $5.50
212-239-1022(NY)
305-371-4666(FLA)

Closeout-All Printed
Baseball Jerseys $1.25/pc

Sweatshirts $3.00/pc
also Plain T's-Adults/kids 696-5586

COMPUTER TAPE
Forty 1000' hubs. Used once/degaused. $10 ea/best offer

Electronic converters; obtain sound movies w/silent movie camera, 200 @ $6.50 ea/best offer 516-239-8462

CEILING FANS
52" cane blades, 3 spd. reversible, 10 yr warrty, antique brass, includes life kit. $59.00 ea, 100 min. Call Steve 214-552-3936 Dallas, TX

PIAGET & ROLEX
STYLE WATCHES
$15
MARK TIME   (212)226-2548

FASHION RINGS
All HGE starting at $1. Way below wholesale prices. Call 216-581-9903

EAR CUFFS!
HOT new item, sterling & gold-filled, over 75 styles. 516/781-6029 eves

CUSTOM TAILOR-GOING OUT OF BUSINESS-HAS LOTS OF 1ST CLASS WOOLS TO SELL.   988-2254

NEW LOOK ¾ sleeve Sweatshirt $36/doz; tee shirts $22-$23/doz; Rags $18/doz. 50/50 Amer made (516)667-7620

SELL to 26,000 FLEA MARKET VENDORS MONTHLY. Advertised in Marketer's Forum mag. 516-829-5275.

JORDACHE

& Other Major Brands, designer & basic Jeans for kids & adults. Corduroy Jeans & Outer Wear. Fall Tops—many styles. UPS/COD Open 7 days.
BW Distributors-Fashion Apparel
Call Toll-Free
800-233-3646
In NJ call
201-367-0708

CASSETTE 'Walkman $13
w/Hotline & Rewind

AM/FM Clock Radio $13.00
EQUALIZER 300 watt 7-band LED $21
HEADPHONES for 'Walkman' ... $1.65
PRINTING Calc Nrml Paper From $14
SHARP Portable Stereo $52
VIDEO Comp/Game w/cartridge .. $38
HAIR DRYER 1600 watt $4.95
TIMEX Clock $5.50
All Kinds of 'Walkman' Radios
Call For Large-Quantity Price
119 W.30 St NYC   212-564-0567

SUNGLASS CLOSEOUTS

GLASS CASES-SEWING KITS-NAIL BRUSHES-BILLFOLDS-PURSE MIRRORS-DIARIES-KEYCASES-LIGHTERS-LINED RUBBER GLOVES-SHOWER CAPS - COMBS - KEY CHAINS-WHISTLES-STICKERS
JOSEPH ZIFF co Inc 61W23 929-6800

CULT PEARLS W/14KT GOLD

Studs; 5mm $21; 6mm $25; 7mm $36;
Pearls on 15" chain; w/4 pearls $42;
w/FW pearls/14K beads $33; w/8 pearls $45; w/7mm pend $36. Sample 4pcs $109. COD or MO to:
Oyster Imports, PO BOX 55,
Commack, NY 11725

ATTENTION: RESTAURANT/DELI/BAR OWNERS

We have a special deal on trashbags. The're packed 2000 to a box. Your cost $99.99 (5c each). For delivery call
609-234-3966

DIRECT FROM FACTORY !!!
BELOW WHOLESALE PRICE

New Fall Line Available. Jogging Suits, Jeans, Blouses, Men's Shirts, Jkts, Polyester Lounge Wear, & Sweaters. Call 212-492-0301.

VIDEO GAMES FOR SALE

We specialize in new & used games that are proven moneymakers. In exc cond. w/good trade-in value at the lowest prices avail. Call 212-458-5005.

CLOSEOUT

Cubic Zirconia Earrings boxed 50c, 100 prs. Earrings $10, Diamond Earrings in Lucite box $15, plus fantastic replica watches. 201-376-0510.

LCD WATCH...:MUSIC CARD

All watches from $1.50. After-sale service. Open Saturday. Also UPS
All quality cards $1.15   212-431-6945
WORLD CLASS SOCCER BALLS & other Sport Goods from Pakistan. Contact Barkat, 212-507-6027; 831-0097
Coll grad seeks entry level position in banking, mkting or advertising. Previous work exp. 865-4884, M-F morn

T-SHIRTS 50/50 U.S. MADE
Muscle T's, schimels from $23.50.
Custom screen printing also available.
COLLAGE 468-3100.

AM/FM WLKMAN-$7.50 buy the case.
Case lot 40 pieces, DEPENDABLE Industries, 820 4th Ave, Bklyn, NY 11232. 212-788-7912/0277

LADIES 2 PC SUITS $6.
Blouses $3, Sweaters $3 & more.
Adams Fashions 201-332-9723.

14 KT GOLD
BELOW WHOLESALE
CHAINS $3.75
SAMPLE ORDER OF POPULAR STYLE CHAINS $100
32 PAGE CATALOG $3-REFUNDABLE WITH YOUR 1ST ORDER
Call or write Box 1962, NY NY 10185
1-800-962-1294   201-869-7799

150,000
W/GIRLST 2 PCS.
SETS BY UNDEROOS

Wonder Woman print.All 1st. qual. Reg. whoselsale:$3.37/set.Our price: $15/Doz. Sizes XS,S,M,L. ideal For Large Discounters, Chain Stores, Jobbers, Exporters, Flea Marketeers, Children's Shops, Fund Raisers, etc. Special Price Consideration For Lge. Qty. By Buyers.Will Ship COD,UPS, Samples $2 Unit.(212)592-3100;
(212)594-3303 or (201) 792-3033

JEANS

Jordache, Gloria Vanderbilt, Sergio, Sasson, Klein's, BonJour, Chardon $10.50. Short Sets, Jogging Outfits, Sundresses $1.85, Blouses & Tops, T-Shirts, Jersies, Rompers, Pants, Seruchi & Members Only style jackets, bathing suits 201-530-8750

TOYS!TOYS!TOYS!

Closeouts/Bargains/Huge line
Flea Mkts! Auctioneers! Bazaars!
Cash & Carry Any Quantities
PROMOTIONAL INDUSTRIES
200 Fifth Ave, NYC 10010
Rm 509   212-924-4470   wkdays 9-5
212-563-3888 for free sam copy.

COLG & COSM CLOSE OUT

All name brand cosmetics, perfumes, treatments, brushes, combs, hair access. NEW SHIPMENTS DAILY.
JANCO DISTR. LI, NY
516/273-7100

OVER 200 BRANDS

Of off-price apparel are available in every issue of OFF-PRICE RETAILING, the way to reach 10,000 stores. Call 212-563-3888 for free sam copy.

CORDUROY PANTS

Gloria Vanderbilt Jeans. Well below wholesale price. Ask for Maria, 279-0516/0517. 1350 B'way, Rm 1606, NY NY 10018

FACTORY WAREHOUSE
NAME BRAND OUTLET

1st qual mdse-all winter styles & fashions, whlse prices 201-991-9223 Danny

Sleepwear, pajamas, panties. We have the famous nightshirt CATHY at low, low price. Craft, 50 Bond St, Dept 260, NY NY 10012. 212-777-6916
PAINTERS CAPS custom printed $15/dz. Cat available. Tim's T-Shirts. Box N, Wilton, NH 03086 VISA/MC accepted. 603-654-2874

$4, $5, $6, $7
Full line ladies, XL's, Jr's, Kids, sweaters, jogs, mini's. Samples UPS/COD: 516-221-6256   914-693-0256

PAINTED EARINGS
Lrg selection of styles & colors, $2-2.50 dz 212-279-6350

WATCHES
LCDs $1.40, stick-ons $1.00.
Call 212-375-5141

43

TOPLINE SALES

Watersnake, folding sunglasses, velco wallet, light-up flower, snake cube, light-up sunvisor, pullback car, turn over buggy, bag key chain, shoe lace, friendship pin, diamond cut sunglasses, reg fashion sunglasses, bo toys, electronic games, super sac, light-up bowtie, lipstick, nailpolish, nail cream, umbrella, and many other variety items with a closeout or quanify price offer.
Call: (212)686-9651 or 686-9652

PHONES
$5.99

(1000—5000 QUANTITIES)
CALL 212-242-8527 MR RICHARDS

.....MFR's CONNECTION.....
Flea Marketers:
Sweaters, size 7-18—$18/dz. Blouses size 7-14—$24/dz. Tops & Blouses size 4-14—$42/dz. Skirts & Pants—$48/dz. Cord Blazers—$66/dz. Velour Jog Suits—$168 to $216/dz. · Genuine Leather Coats—$360/dz.
UPS-All States   (201)477-0900

ATT: FLEA MKT OPERS
STORE OWNERS, SCHOOLS
& ORGANIZATIONS

We have the best prices on painter's caps & rock mirrors. Also we will do custom design logos. Call us for a quote! (201)780-2420 weekdays

CUBIC ZIRCONIA
$.67/CT

1.00/ct q.f. earrings $4
1.00/ct 14kt earrings $12
MARC X 212-929-6240

JEWELRY CLOSEOUT

Moving Must Sell Immed Imported Italian costume necklaces (mostly beaded), bracelets, pins, earrings,bulk chain,many styles & colors. Storage bins also avail. 914-946-8000

JEWELRY

Quality sterling silver & genuine turquoise earrings $1.50/pr, pendants $1.10/ea, rings $1.25. Color catalog. $25.00 sample COD. 800-392-2532

60M NEW GARMENTS 40cEA

Sub & teen girls sizes 5-14. Shorts, walking shorts, pants & tops. Most 100% cotton gab. twill. Sun & Mon 516-938-1300, Other 212-847-3600

FLASHING VISOR

Headbands, bow ties, feather clips, lighter covers, costume jewelry, necklaces. Call George, 212-594-3022.

WIPING CLOTHES

Absorbant cotton for busn/hm. Dark and lite colors, 10lb min. order
212-674-8873/518-842-1210.

SCREWS & BOLTS

Mfg plant going out of busn. Hundreds of thousands avail. All zink plated. Call for free samples. 516-746-3668

POSTER CLOSEOUT

Full line color/B&W imports. $300/thou, 1 thou; $250/thou, 5 thou; $200/thou, 10 thou. Call 212-592-9788.

BEAUTIFUL GEORGETTE DRESSES
From $9.50   Retail Value $30-80
Min. $50 samples
Call (212)526-2217

CHAPTER FIVE

TWELVE HOURS OF FUN —
TO MAKE $3,000 OR $10,000 IN PROFITS

I have been to Las Vegas time and time again, trying to create a system to win at the numerous games of chance—to be precise, any game of chance. I have tried Craps, the dice game played in more countries in the world than any other, from the back allies of Harlem in New York City, to the gold-laced tables in Monte Carlo.

I have tried Roulette, the game for Kings and Queens, that seems to be more popular, now days, with the ladies than with the men. I have bet on black and red, odds or evens and even sometimes placed all my money on a favoriet 35-to-1 shot. I have never won more than $500 and I will never get used to people leaning over my shoulder to place a one-time bet.

I have sat at the Blackjack tables (or 21 as some gamblers perfer to call it) for twelve to fifteen hours at a crack. I have read all the books on how to beat the dealer at 21, and have tried all the systems of counting cards there are on the market.

Then there are the Slot Machines. I have played the dollar and five dollar slot machines for hours on end, in fact so long one Saturday morning, that my hands turned black and it took several washings and almost two cakes of soap to clean them.

Not to mention the frustration piled upon frustration. It seemed like any and all the slot machines I tried I always seemed to come out a loser. I remember being up $2,000 one evening, but like always I ended up not only losing all my winnings but several thousand dollars I had brought with me.

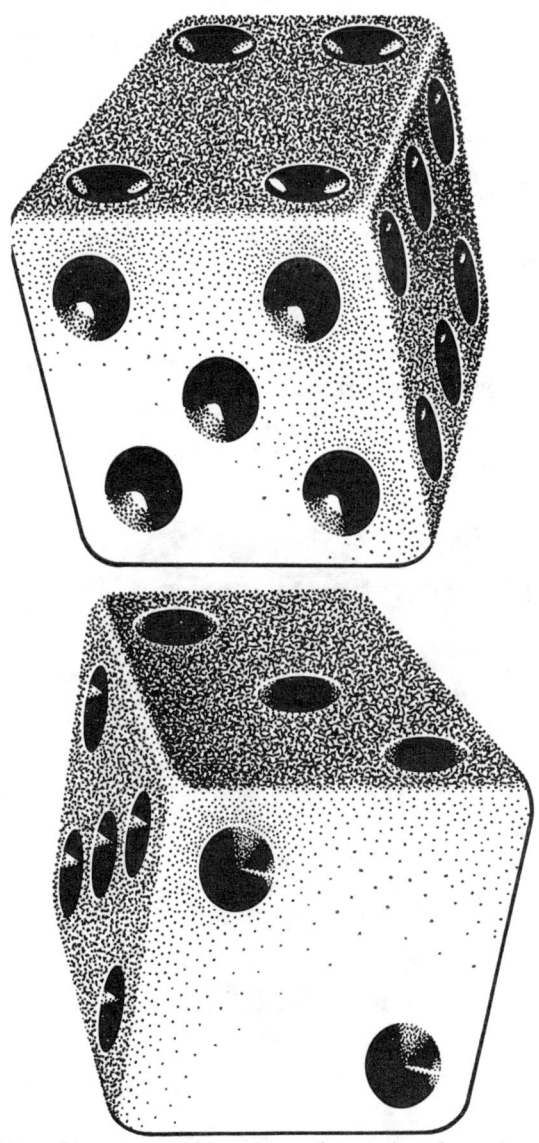

Then there was that marvelous day last August, when I thought I was really onto something. I thought I had finally figured out a way to beat the slot machines. I was going from machine to machine winning $100, $200, and even $500 jackpots. I even carried my luck next store to the Dunes Casino, which in most cases is very hard to do, and was winning at the same speed in their establishment.

My system was so simple, I should have realized it was too good to be true.

The secret was to find one of the change girls and give her five or ten dollars to point me to the right machine. Sure enough, she was always right. Well almost always right. Indeed, I did win several $100 and $500 jackpots. In fact, one day I was so hot that I was up five grand ($5,000) before eleven in the morning.

Then like always, "Greed" set in and I thought I couldn't lose. I found myself moseying over to try my hand at winning the "big money"—the million dollar jackpots.

"Can you guess what happened next? You don't have to guess, I'll tell you." I lost everything and I mean everything!

To make a long story short, I have stopped trying to win at the slot machines. Period!

That brings us to a game that is so boring, so uninspiring, that when I first noticed it, sitting in the far corner of the casino, I thought it was designed for the old and possibly the tired gamblers who just wanted to sit down and rest a while.

During my first encounter with the game, I sat down and was uninterested at what was going on. I played the game haphazardly and was just glad for the chance to rest my feet.

I watched the stewards in charge of the game go through their monotonous, never-ending, ritual of taking in the bets and starting the balls bouncing. As I slowly drifted into a trance, I began to wonder if I hadn't, sometime in the past, encountered this same type of game when I was growing up in a small town in Virginia. The same type of slow, relaxed atmosphere that lends itself to southern hospitality.

Suddenly, without warning, I was awakened. A loud schreeching voice from a woman sitting behind me awoke me and shot me to my feet like someone had just zapped me with 120 volts of electricity. She screamed at the top of her voice..."I WON! I JUST WON $10,000 DOLLARS."

Well, I'll tell you I didn't know at the time, what in the world she was talking about. I thought this game "Keno" was just for suckers. I thought the casinos allowed someone to win a couple of hundred every two or three months just to keep it vaguely interesting.

I watched her intensely while she was collecting her winnings—$10,000 in cash mind you. Finally after about fifteen minutes or so when all the hoopla had died down, I had a chance to talk to her. I asked her if she was surprised that she had won so much money at a game that seemed so unlikely to produce any winners. She informed me in no uncertain terms that she plays this game often and she has won $3,000, $10,000 and even as much as $20,000 every time she comes to Las Vegas.

I was interested to say the least, and I proceeded to pick her brain in the short time I had before I had to catch my plane back to Washington, D.C.

She told me she has been coming to Las Vegas every other month, for the past two years, since she had discovered a flaw in the Keno game. She proceeded to explain to me how the game is played. You see—the game is played with eighty balls that are placed in a large round container, which then is operated with air pressure that gives the balls a bouncing effect. The stewards of the game then draw out one ball at a time until they have drawn out twenty balls. Your entrance into the game is played like bingo. You pick out any number of numbers that you think will make you a winner. This combination of numbers ia then given odds and a dollar amount that you can win. Example: Let's say you pick six numbers: 45, 47, 55, 56, 80, and 10. Then let's assume you bet $2 that the next time they pick 20 numbers from the glass cylinder your six numbers will be among them. If they are, you will win $3,000. If you pick seven numbers and they are picked, you win $10,000—it is that simple.

$10,000 Dollars

Of course we all know it isn't that simple. If it was everyone would be winning at this game called Keno and the casinos would be bankrupt.

Is there a catch to it? Certainly, like always there is a catch to it. Here's the catch. The odds are not in your favor, even though you may think they are, at first glance. The game seems simple and easy to win at. But, after playing it for several hours, here's what happens. First: You become bored with the action and leave; or Second, you get tired of playing the same numbers, continuously game after game, with no results. So your next step is to quit and move on to another game of chance with a little more action. STOP, that's what the casinos are reyling on you to do. Before you do that let me give you a little insight on how to win at this game.

Here's what the lady who had just won $10,000 told me. She said she found a flaw in the mechanical operation of the game. A flaw brings the odds more in your favor. The casinos are not aware of this flaw, but even if they were it would be very difficult for them to change it.

Here's the Secret. The game is played with eighty balls, as I previously discussed and twenty balls are drawn out each and every game. (Something like bingo.) And the winners are paid after each game. (NOTE: You must be there after each game is played to collect. Once a new game is in progress, the previous game is void.) Now here's how it works. Each ball is a "ping pong" ball, you know, the ones like your child plays with when he or she plays Ping Pong, or table tennis as it is called on the west coast. Each and every ball is supposed to be identical, but ironically enough they are not. There is no way a ping pong ball manufacturer can manufacture each and every ball to be exactly the same size and weight. Although they all look and feel the same they are not. Each ball is slightly different in weight or size. Which, by the way, can not be noticed with the naked eye.

As the game is put into action you find that the balls are blown around in a large round cylinder made of glass or plastic. All eighty balls are suspended and are blown around and around for about five mintunes before the game commences. While watching the balls being drawn out one at a time, game after game, you will find some of the balls are lighter than the others which will cause them to be drawn out more often than the others. Your job is to determine which balls are lighter and to pick out six or seven of the lightest ones to bet on. (I will tell you later why six and seven is the wise bet.) This can some times be time consuming and difficult to determine. But if you are willing to devote 12 hours at playing Keno, nonstop action, don't worry about going to the bathroom or eating, there will be ample time to satisfy your personal needs and to enjoy lunch or dinner between games. Besides, most hotels that feature Keno as one of their attractions offer Keno in the dining room. Most even have runners to take your bets. If you will follow this method, religiously, for twelve hours I will guarantee that you will win up to $3,000 or $10,000 for your efforts. But remember, once you start your play, you can not change your numbers or miss one game during this 12-hour period. If you do you will reduce your odds and will have to start over again.

If you play six numbers at let's say Cesaer's Palace, placing a $2 bet each time, you will win almost $3,000 each time you win. If you play seven numbers you will win nearly $10,000.

The reason for playing six or seven numbers is the odds.

Greater odds in your favor to be exact. After calcullating the odds on the different games offered in Keno you will determine, as I did, that six or seven numbers is your best bet for winning the most money in any given twelve hour sitting.

Keep in mind that each Casino will have different balls and a slightly different machine that rotates the balls, and if one of the balls has the misfortune to break then it is your job to determine if this new ball, newly inserted into the game, is lighter or heavier than the others. If it turns out that this ball is lighter than you will have to place it into your game plan.

An opportunity like this may sound too good to be true, but it's not.

The opportunity exists in Las Vegas —an exciting, fast paced, high profit town where you can perhaps leverage your small investment, with this system—into $10,000.00 quickly!

Consider This Fact:

★ You can begin with only $200-$500 out of pocket investment yet earn winnings from a single twelve hour sitting in the $3,000-$10,000 range or higher.

In summary, it's an ideal method for anyone who wants a high profit venture, and a hassle-free life every month of the year, from gambling.

Of course, just like any other business it does have a few risks. But, I think you'll see the risk element of this game Keno is perhaps much less than the average business venture. The risk is that you can lose a modest amount of time an money, but that's your only loss. The advantage is that you might find a new way of life, without stress.

One of the best features of my system is that you don't need any real starting capital to speak of. You can begin with as little as a few hundred dollars. Second, you can do this quietly and discreetly without quitting your job or disrupting your other business activities.

You don't need any elaborate experience or skill —just a desire to win and the willingness to give my new system a shot.

Living the life of leisure is actually a simple and exciting way of life that can be mastered by following a few simple rules I have layed out in this chapter.

Good Luck, and give this system a fair try. I think you will experence, after twelve hours of play, maybe shorter, a pleasent surprise.

CHAPTER SIX

A $500,000 A YEAR BUSINESS,
WITH LITTLE OR NO INVESTMENT!

The market for courier/cargo services is any business or individual that needs to have any item transported within the range that you have chosen to operate. The type of courier and cargo services that will be discussed here includes metro area or localized (as opposed to nationwide) deliveries. Courier services generally carry flat parcels such as contracts, proposals, and letters from one office to another or to an airport within the same city or metro area. Cargo services in this case are those that operate in the same range, but carry larger parcels, usually weighing under 200 pounds. The ranges for these services characteristically cover a commercial area which would take a few hours to drive from one end to the other.

In addition to this wide-open market, courier/cargo service is attractive because it is not burdened by Department of Transportation or Interstate Commerce Commission regulations. The only requirement is that your business be registered or licensed by your state Commerce Commission which costs less than $10 and requires minimal paperwork. Therefore, with a minimal amount of equipment and a small investment, you can develop a solid customer base in your own courier/cargo service. In other words, for anyone offering reliable, efficient service, the sky is the limit!

To begin with, you have to choose the size of parcels that you will or will not carry and the range in which you choose to operate. These choices will determine the type of vehicle you need. Additional equipment required will be a phone, a bellboy or two-way radio and a dolley or hand truck if you're planning to haul anything larger than envelopes. The personnel you'll need will be a dispatcher and a driver.

The size of items you choose to carry might be partially determined by your market. For example, a high rise office corridor would probably be sending more envelopes than parcels. A manufacturing community, on the other hand, would probably be moving parcels more frequently. At any rate, a small station wagon will do for courier service but if you plan to carry parcels, a van is a necessity. The small wagon might be easy on gas but the van will help you keep customers satisfied when they need larger or greater numbers of parcels delivered.

When you choose the range that you will be operating within, consider that anything outside "commercial zones" (as defined by the Interstate Commerce Commission) is regulated by ICC. These zones are determined by population concentrations and by mileage. To find out whether or not your delivery range falls within a commercial zone, and would therefore be exempt from regulations, you can write or call:

Interstate Commerce Commission
12th St. and Constitution Ave.
Public Assistance Branch
Room 2147
Washington, DC 20423

(202) 275-7863

This office can also put you in touch with your state Commerce Commission for licensing information.

Once you have decided on the range and the type of service you will offer, you can explore your options in getting a vehicle. You can buy your own, lease one or hire a driver who owns his own vehicle. The latter option, which is common practice in the industry, is probably the most sensible approach for a newcomer. When you subcontract the driving, you do not have to keep payroll books which are costly and time-consuming recordkeeping. With drivers the payments could be based on commission (up to 50%), or the driver could be paid a flat weekly rate, or be paid based on mileage traveled.

While each driver should be required to present a certificate of insurance proving that he is covered for commercial driving, cargo insurance can be taken out by the driver or by you as the company owner. Cargo insurance is not mandatory, but is advisable and can cost anywhere from $500 to $1,000 per year per vehicle. The factors influencing the rate are the type of cargo being carried, the type of vehicle used and the range of travel.

Remember when hiring, that a driver is more than just a driver; he is a reflection on your company. Select only those people who you feel best represent you in appearance and manner. There is no place for a sloppy or short-tempered driver who might quickly destroy the goodwill you have worked to establish with clients. A good driver is a good advertisement for your company and should be courteous and pleasant to clients.

The vehicle belonging to the driver should also fall under similar scrutiny. While some clients may not seem to care what the vehicle looks like, as long as their delivery is made on time, some will give their business to your competitors whose fleet gives a better impression. Remember that a battered, rusted van does not inspire confidence or portray an image of efficiency and reliability which is essential to maintain in the courier/cargo business.

A bellboy system or two-way radio is the next necessity to be obtained. The local phone company and private firms in most metropolitan areas offer bellboy services. The dispatcher, when he receives a call, dials the phone number which rings the driver's bellboy unit. The driver then goes to the nearest phone and calls the dispatcher to find out where his next pickup should be. The effectiveness of this system can be maximized if drivers are trained to carry map, pad and pen to the phone in order to minimize errors made in receiving directions and addresses.

Although many courier/cargo services start out with bellboys, they eventually, when affordable, purchase or lease two-way radios. This saves time for drivers who do not have to find a phone and a parking place in order to receive their next instruction.

The last essential that has not been discussed is the dispatcher, a key figure in the success of your business. The dispatcher who knows his territory can efficiently arrange pickups and drops and give your business the competitive edge. Your clients will notice the speed with which you are able to make pickups and you will be saving money on gas.

So, with all the basic equipment and personnel in place, your range and type of service decided, how do you go about getting yourself known? The primary choices are media advertising, direct mailings, networking, Yellow Page ads and signs on your vehicles.

The effectiveness of media advertising will be determined by the newspaper you choose to advertise in and the look or design of your ad. Designing a professional looking ad that can be used several times will help keep advertising costs to a minimum. Direct mail, on the other hand, is more costly up front, but you can target a very specific audience by purchasing the right mailing lists from list brokers. Be sure that your direct mailing card or brochure is not dated, because it may cost you anywhere from 10 to 15 cents each for a postcard mailer to 50 to 75 cents each for a brochure if you have 10,000 printed. A word of warning...the more you have printed, the less expensive per piece, but if you don't have the cash to mail as many as you print, you're not saving any money.

Bulk mailing permits from the post office cost an additional $40 per year. The only requirement is that you mail 200 pieces at one time, sorted by zip codes and that they be stamped with your permit number. Sorting into zip codes would be a good job for your dispatcher to do in between calls.

Networking, the personal way to make yourself known, is yet another means of developing a strong customer base. While this requires some energy and charisma, there is no substitute for personal contact with potential customers. Dropping by to see them at intervals will help personalize your service and make them feel comfortable calling you when they need something delivered.

Finally, placing signs on your vehicles is another means of advertising. Magnetic or lettered signs (depending on whether you subcontract or have your own vehicles) should display the company name and logo, the phone number (large enough to read) and any specialty that you might offer such as "same-day service" or "open 24 hours." If you do use signs, make sure your drivers don't forget that they are "flying the company colors." A harried, discourteous driver on the road can turn off other drivers who might be potential customers.

Once you have established a solid customer base, you can begin to look for larger contracts. While getting a large contract might double or triple the size of a fledgling business, it is best not to put all your eggs in one basket. Take on bigger contracts, but balance them against your solid customer base, never letting any single contract exceed the volume of business on which you could continue operating if you were to lose your "big fish." Consider contracting with a company like Flying Tigers that subs out the running of its local offices in many areas.

Like in any other business, good management of your courier/cargo service will result in good cash flow. Billing clients on a weekly basis is the best way to promote good cash flow, especially since most businesses operate on a 30 to 45 day payment schedule. Offering a discount of whatever you feel you can afford also stimulates cash flow and makes clients feel as if they are getting a special deal.

At any given time deciding on the number of drivers you need can be tricky. Ideally you have few enough drivers to have plenty of work for them, which makes them happy and which makes them stay with you longer, but you have enough drivers to efficiently satisfy your clients' needs.

Using these guidelines for starting your own courier/cargo service, you should be able to operate your new business, establishing a solid customer base and then expand at whatever rate your market will allow and at whatever rate you feel you can accommodate growth. Further general business information can be obtained from the Small Business Administration which offers seminars and business counseling through its regional and local offices. Call or write:

Small Business Administration
Office of Public Communication
1441 L Street, N.W.
Washington, DC 24416
(202) 653-6822

If you are interested in renting a Van on a daily basis, call HERTZ Truck rental and apply for their credit card. It is not that hard to qualify for and it can perhaps increase your business tenfold, without the expense of buying or permanently leasing a van in the beginning stage.

Hertz: 800-654-3131
PS: The Hertz Credit Card can also be used for car rental in any part of the country.

CHAPTER SEVEN

START YOUR OWN COMPANY FOR A SONG
AND MAKE $3,000 A MONTH FOR SINGING.

The first singing telegram was delivered to entertainer Rudy Vallee as a birthday surprise on July 28, 1933. Soon messengers throughout the nation were melodizing their messages. Although the popularity of singing telegrams eventually waned, they began making a strong comeback in the late 70s.

The resurgence continues, thanks largely to a number of innovations. It is still possible, of course, to hire messengers who wear the traditional bellboy uniform, but modern singing messengers often appear dressed as gorillas, belly dancers, devils, clowns or in nearly any other costume imaginable. And some messengers wear almost nothing at all by the time they finish their routines.

More often than not, messengers add a personal touch by singing lyrics that are based on information supplied by the person paying for the telegram. To further enliven the festivities, customers can also arrange for messengers to leave behind gifts such as helium-filled balloons, plaques, cakes and flowers.

The singing telegram industry is becoming more and more competitive, but plenty of room remains for enterprising newcomers. Anybody can form one of the companies on a shoestring; you don't need much more than enthusiasm, determination and a strong desire to make people happy.

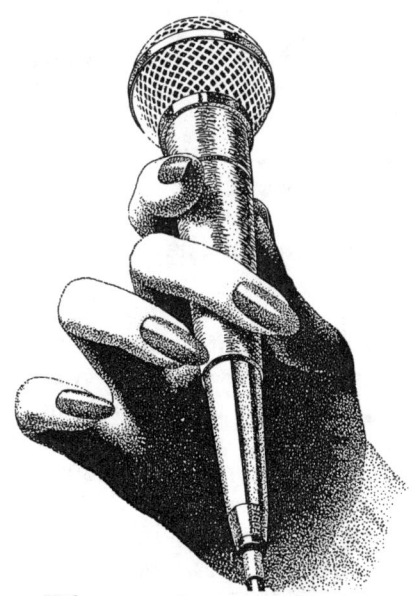

When you are starting out, you may find that a spare bedroom provides ample office space. In fact, a number of singing telegram companies continue to operate from owners' homes long after becoming successful.

Caught up in the excitement of embarking on a new business, you will perhaps be tempted to advertise extensively. Try to resist. Explains Joanne Barry, owner of Dittygrams, "I used to advertise all over the place. Then I realized that I had to do a whole lot of Dittygrams just to pay for the advertisements."

Her advice: Forget everything except the Yellow Pages.

Check to see how other singing telegram services advertise in the Yellow Pages. If they are running large ads, you should consider buying more than a line or two in order to be competitive. In any case, there is probably little need to run an ad that is larger than 2½ inches tall by one column wide.

The most effective advertising sometimes costs nothing. It comes in the form of free publicity from various media. For example, Jeff Gerhold, who owns and operates Croonatune, received some timely publicity immediately before Valentine's Day when he was interviewed over the telephone for a radio show, listed as a "best buy" in *Washingtonian* magazine, a feature in a segment of PM Magazine, a nationally syndicated television show.

In Gerhold's case, the reporters contacted him initially. Sometimes, though, you may have to give the media a little nudge.

Spend some time thinking of angles to get your company publicized. One proven method involves calling a popular television or radio station and volunteering to make a free on-the-air appearance to help celebrate the birthday of one of the station's stars.

Once you've lined up one of these publicity stunts, assign the job to your most talented messenger. Or, if you work alone, be prepared to perform like you've never performed before. You will never have a better audience of potential customers, so make certain that your company's name is mentioned in the introduction or song.

Getting publicity through newspapers and local magazines is also relatively easy. Editors, always on the lookout for new ideas, might welcome your suggestion that a reporter could write an interesting story after accompanying you on your rounds. (Perhaps you could give the reporter a costume and a small, temporary part in the act.)

Don't expect immediate response from whatever media coverage you are able to drum up. You merely need to make a strong enough impression that people will remember you and look you up in the phone book when special occasions arise.

Until those calls start coming in regularly, your budding singing telegram service is likely to be a one-person operation. Because you can't be out delivering telegrams and answering yhour phone at the same time, you will probably want to purchase an answering machine. Serviceable machines are available for as little as $100.

If you called Jeff Gerhold at Croonatune, and you'll hear a recorded message of him singing, "More than the greatest love the world has known, I'll croon a tune for you right in their home." Then he briefly describes the service and asks callers to leave a name and phone number.

Gerhold, who delivers his singing messages primarily over the phone, can tap in to his answering machine with a remote apparatus when he is away from home. Consequently, he is even able to sing messages from hotel rooms during his vacations.

Larger companies also make use of taped messages. Dittygrams, for instance, has a separate line for a demonstration tape that includes snippets from various acts. Dittygrams' Joanne Barry produces new tapes from time to time to keep the public interested.

Like Gerhold, Barry worked alone at first. But soon she had more business than she could handle.

By then she knew exactly what to look for when selecting fellow messengers. "You have to be able to hush up a room as soon as you start," she says. "When you go into a restaurant, you should be loud enough to entertain everybody, not just one table of people. And as you leave, flood the place with business cards."

Another criterion Barry emphasizes is physical attractiveness. "Everybody has to look good, especially the strippers," she says.

Appearances are less important at Gertie Gorilla-Gram. After all, once inside a gorilla suit and a pink tutu, everyone looks pretty much alike. Personality counts for more than anything else as far as owner Marilynn Bellmann is concerned.

"I see Gertie as a loveable, fun-loving gorilla that doesn't get insulting or rude," says Bellmann. "She has to do lots of ad libbing."

It seems that Gertie is also thoughtful. She always leaves behind a toy stuffed gorilla. Attached to its neck by a colorful ribbon is a card with the words to the original song she has performed.

Great gorillas are made, not born, insists Bellmann. Her recruits all undergo "gorilla training" in simulated situations before being turned loose on the public.

"We depend on word-of-mouth advertising and repeat business, so we have to give a consistent, quality product," she says.

Many performers who work for singing messenger companies are independent contractors. Pay varies, but they often receive half of what they bring in. Some owners feel that commissioned messengers have more incentive than salaried employees to put on a good show because they, too, are trying to build business. They yearn to have their acts specifically requested by customers.

Brad Doan, owner of Candy Man Telegrams, uses both full-time salaried and part-time commissioned messengers. He is comfortable with either system.

"What you have to remember is that people who want to get out in front of the public are fairly theatrical anyway," he says. "They're not doing it just for the money."

Indeed, dinner theatre actors and actresses, drama students from local colleges, moonlighting music teachers and other people with performing backgrounds have become the mainstays of many successful singing telegram companies. Likewise, you can quickly enhance the reputation of your new business by hiring such polished performers.

Look for versatility. The ideal candidate can carry a tune, dance, juggle, do imitations, play a half dozen musical instruments, perform magic, create balloon animals and uncomplainingly slip into even the most ridiculous of costumes.

Of course, you may have trouble discovering such a being, but you don't have to settle for the first person who walks through the door, either. Larry Balsamo, owner of Haywires, estimates that he hires about one out of 30 people who audition for him.

Harder to evaluate than talent but equally important is reliability. Your customers expect punctual, professional service and they deserve nothing less. Therefore, you should always have contingency plans. Make it clear to your messengers that you expect them to notify you promptly if they ever anticipate problems in meeting their obligations. Even when you have messengers you feel are dependable, a time may come when you find yourself filling in for one of them at the last moment.

For the most part, though, the messengers you hire will make life easier for you. A new messenger often will bring freshness to an act that was beginning to grow stale.

You may find that one of your messengers is willling to help with some of the writing chores. You'll probably need it because, as Haywire's Larry Balsamo explains, "the typical singing telegram company uses at least twice as much material as a Broadway musical."

A number of companies benefit from having a performer that is also handy with a needle and thread. That's a great way to hold down the cost of costumes, which can be one of your biggest expenses.

If you don't have the luxury of a seamstress on staff, you will want to take steps to keep that expense in check. Shop around for the best price. One costume shop sells a perfectly suitable gorilla suit for approximately $100, whereas a competitor's prices range from $300 to $1,500. For outfits worn by characters such as French maids, bellboys, or policemen, a uniform supply store may offer more durable, less expensive merchandise than a costume shop.

Avoid renting costumes whenever possible. It usually costs as much to rent one two or three times as it does to buy it.

Keep in mind the cost of costumes and other expenses when establishing your prices. Certain expenses such as special cakes and mileage for deliveries far from your office can be passed on directly to the customers as a surcharge.

However, if you have become well known for the little extra touches you provide, you may want to include them as part of the package. Candy Man Telegrams, for example, always delivers two dozen helium-filled balloons with the performance, all for $38.50.

Once owner Brad Doan buys the balloons, he has to spend about 30 cents to fill each one with helium, and the price of the gas climbs continually. He says that the impact of the balloons makes the expense worthwhile for him.

Regardless of the type of service you provide, you should charge at least $29 for a singing telegram that is delivered in person, according to Haywire's Larry Balsamo. Rates for his company's singing telegrams range from $29 to $75.

Charge more for acts that require more than one messenger. Recently Joanne Barry assembled a complete cast for a special 45-minute presentation. Sponsoring the $700 dittygram was a Florida businessman who wanted to give his wife an anniversary present she would never forget.

Barry says that she encourages customers to use her dual acts by giving price breaks. The most popular of these acts is a comedy stripper, followed by a serious stripper. "We try to keep it tasteful," she adds.

To get an idea of how much you should charge, scout out your competition. If your prices are too high in comparison, you may lose business.

Jeff Gerhold had the opposite problem at Croonatune. At $10 for a telephoned singing message, his services were underpriced. He raised his fee to $29 and suddenly found himself much busier.

"People just wanted to spend more than $10 for their loved ones," he reasons.

His point is a good one. Clearly, the heightened success of the singing telegram industry indicates that many people are willing to pay top dollar to surprise and delight their family, friends or business associates. Give them what they want and your business will thrive.

BALLOONS WHOLESALE

Belle Arbor
252 Eastern Parkway
Farmingdale, New York 11735
We ship anywhere!

Ad-Venture Plus
104 E 40th Street
New York, NY
Free Catalog!
Imprinted Balloons!

COSTUMES WHOLESALE

House of Costumes
166 Jericho Turnpike
Long Island, NY
516-294-0170
Visa, Mastercard Accepted

Universal Costumes
1540 Broadway, 17th floor
New York, NY
Costumes made to order!

Examples of "Yellow Pages" Advertising:

EASTERN ONION
SINGING TELEGRAMS

Delivered in Person by our Talented Costumed Messengers

The Unusual Gift for that Special Someone
Select from more than 95 Original, Professional,
Funny Musical Performances & Unique Gifts
for All Occasions

- French Maid
- Amazon Woman
- Fairy Onion
- Amazon Man
- Mae East
- Pink Gorilla
- Scarlet O'Piglett
- Super Onion Man
- Wonder Onion Woman
- Bellygram
- Rhapsody in Balloons

Made My Day

OFFICES COAST TO COAST
Call 6 Days - 8 AM to 6 PM

752-3773

8000 E. GIRARD AV. DENVER

CHAPTER EIGHT

RENT-A-GAME, AND MAKE $68,000
THE FIRST YEAR!

A New Idea, that puts you in on the ground floor of a brand new business.

America is a nation of game players. For years manufacturers, distributors and retailers have been making billions of dollars providing the amusements that challenge and keep Americans happy. Now, with the advent of electronic games and video game cartridges, the responsibility of keeping America's game players happy has become a much more expensive proposition. But it's also opened the door for the entrepreneur to step inside the lucrative game market and get a big slice of those billions of dollars being spent each year. In fact, a wise entrepreneur can parlay $10,000 into nearly $68,000 in one year!

The entrepreneur owes this opportunity to the advancements in microtechnology and the introduction of the home computer. Computers cost hundreds and even thousands of dollars plus the costly components which make them more versatile. The game cartridges that make home computers so attractive to the game player are expensive, too. Electronic games are also expensive. This presents a problem to game players, young and old. The percentage of income Americans have been spending on their home games and amusements has not increased, yet the cost of their games has greatly increased. Americans just haven't got the money to spend on the same quantity of new games that they have spent in the past. Simply translated: The game player cannot have every game he wants. Not if he has to buy it.

The cost of electronic games makes this clear. For instance, even at discount prices, the retailer can expect to spend the following amounts:

Ms. Pac Man Tabletop Arcade	$39.97
Snoopy Tennis	$19.97
Pocket Simon	$21.97
Sensory Chess Challenger	$131.50
Electronic Backgammon	$29.50
Electronic Baseball	$32.90
Merlin	$29.96
Simon	$27.97
Electronic Battleship	$32.90

These are just a few of the hundreds of electronic games now on the market.

The same situation exists with discounted video cartridge games. For example:

Keystone Kapers	$31.95
Centipede	$31.95
Dungeons & Dragons	$27.95
Super Cobra	$25.95
Robot Tank	$24.97
Turbo	$24.97
Zaxxon	$37.90
Black Jack/Poker	$27.90
Smurf	$27.90

Again, this is just a small sample of what's available.

Even at discount prices, how many parents can afford to purchase all the electronic games and cartridges they and their children want to enjoy? In addition, most children's boredom threshold is very low. The game or cartridge that they insisted was a necessity on Monday often has lost its appeal and sits unused by the following Sunday.

There is a simple solution to this problem. Instead of buying games, rent them. What? You say you can't rent electronic games and cartridges? Maybe not now you can't but if you act quickly you can not only rent these costly items but you can be on the ground floor of a new and very lucrative business venture.

Entering the Rent-A-Game business is not complicated. The most important and primary element is location. A storefront of approxiamately 632 square feet will suffice, but to be successful it must be on the "beaten path." You'll want it to be in the type of (strip) shopping center that draws grocery and pharmacy shoppers. This will provide you with continual traffic and plenty of parking. It should also be located in a highly populated area of your city. You're establishing a first, so you'll want to be within reach of as many people as possible.

The store needn't be fancy. In fact, the plainer the better. And keep your initial investment as low as possible. A suitable store in a good location should be available for $2000 up front and that should include the sign for your business.

Do not try to outfit your store with all new equipment. Shop "going out of business" sales, "close-outs," and used office furniture warehouses. If you can find a store that really is selling out you should be able to make a good deal on most of the equipment and office accessories you'll need. You'll definitely need a cash register, but get it as economically as possible. An L-shaped counter with under-the-counter storage area is another necessity. Purchase one as large as the entrance area to your store will accommodate.

The shelving for your games and cartridges should be simple. If you must purchase them, again try to get them used. If you're handy with a hammer and nails, you'll save even more money. Constructing your own shelving will also enable you to customize them to exactly fit your needs. You could spend as little as $350 on this basic need. If you're not a do-it-yourselfer, you may still be able to save money by purchasing the materials and hiring someone to do the labor. This will, of course, increase the cost several hundred dollars.

Arrange your shelving around three walls of your store with your entrance and counter area at the front. This will reduce your need for a sophisticated security system. This arrangement will make your stock visible from the counter area and the clerk at the counter can easily observe everyone entering and leaving the store and also those who are browsing.

To further minimize shoplifting, place only the video cartridge containers on your shelves. When your customer makes his game selection, he simply presents the empty package to the clerk behind the counter. The actual cartridges are filed beneath the counter. It's quick and easy for the clerk to pull the correct cartridge and place it in the container.

Later, when the cardboard containers become worn, you will have to replace them. Vinyl covers are available at $1.10 each. Remove the front of the worn cardboard cover and glue the colorful advertisement to the replacement container for easy identification by the customer. Your distributor can assist you in purchasing these covers.

Personnel is not a problem in this type of business. With an operation of this size, it is only necessary to have two people on duty during any time period. One of these can even be a part-timer. At times, even one person can sufficiently meet the demands of the store. This makes it especially conducive for a family-owned and operated establishment.

The amount of stock you have initially will greatly determine the success or failure of your operation. You must supply what your customer wants. This includes all of the most popular games and cartridges. Those which are the most in demand you should purchase at least two of each. When new customers come into your store it's very important that you make a positive impression by providing them with the game they've been wanting to play or which is the newest on the market. If they go away disappointed, it's a good possibility that they won't come back. A minimum of 80 game cartridges, 70 electronic games and 25 sports games or pieces of equipment should get you off on the right foot.

It's a good idea to visit all the stores in your area which carry games and note the most popular brands. Distributors will be happy to talk to you about their best sellers. Remember, you're a potential customer and will be purchasing your inventory from them. Distributors are located all over the country. Some of the largest and most popular are in Maryland, Ohio, New York and California.

The most economical way to record and control your inventory is with an envelope and card system, similar to those previously used in lending libraries and currently in many video rental stores. Attach three by five envelopes containing standard lined cards on the bottom of your electronic games and on your cartridge containers. When a game is rented, the customer signs the card and the card is then placed in an index file. When the game is returned the card is pulled form the file, the name marked off and the card is returned to the envelope attached to the game and the game returned to stock.

Establish your card file system according to the days of the week and record the expected rental time on the card. All rentals which go out on Monday will immediately be obvious if they haven't been returned within a day or two. It takes only a minute to check to see if the game is overdue. You can then call the customer and remind him the game is due back in the store.

You should also establish a delinquent fee policy. Games which are kept longer than the original agreed-upon rental period should be charged an additional $2.00 per day above the usual daily rental. It encourages prompt return of your merchandise and better control for you. This should be included in the original contract the member signs.

A cash policy is very important. Accept personal checks only with proper identification. Credit cards are great. Ask your bank for Visa & Mastercard applications. Their fee is 3 to 4 percent but it's worth it in the long run. (Don't worry, it's easy to apply for Visa & Mastercard for your business. American Express is another story.) Later, when you've expanded and know your membership better, then, if it's profitable to you, you can consider American Express.

Your initial investment will include the following:

Store and utilities	$2,500
Store equipment	$1,500
Advertising	$ 500
Office and miscellaneous expenses	$ 500
	$5,200
80 game cartridges (average $20 wholesale)	$1,600
70 electronic games (average $25 wholesale)	$1,750
25 sports games or equipment (optional)	$ 625
	$3,975

That's a total expenditure of $9,175. Less than $10,000 to start your own business!

A membership club system will solve any early cash flow problems you may experience. If you offer rental-only on a club plan, you'll immediately bring a large amount of money into your business. If you offer a plan charging each family a fee of $25 to join for one year, you will bring $4,375 into your business if you accept rentals for your full inventory of 175 pieces. Your grand opening should easily produce this membership plus a lengthy waiting list. And this is fresh money you can invest in more inventory which will enable you to allow more people to join your club and further increase your income.

By charging $3.00 first day rental and $1.00 per day for each additional day the game is retained in the customer's possession, you can expect each piece of stock to return $9.00 per week at full rental. It will take less than 2½ weeks for you to recoup the cost of each piece of your stock.

If you remain at a membership of 175 and maintain a rental of 90 percent of your merchandise, you can expect to record the following figures (not including additional enrollment fees):

$ 1,413 per week
$5,652 per month
$67,824 per year

And that's only your first year!

Because you will be dealing with merchandise which is handled primarily by children and teenagers, you must have a redeemable damage contract. This contract should be signed by the parents at the time they join your club. It should agree that the merchandise will be returned in the same condition in which it left your establishment and that damages will be assessed to abused merchandise. This means two major things for you: One, you must maintain your stock in perfect working order, including batteries. Second, you must inspect the merchandise when it is returned and keep a current estimate of its condition on the file card. The customer must agree to the condition of the merchandise prior to taking it from the store. His signature on the withdrawal card is the agreement between the two of you that the game is in acceptable operating condition to both parties.

In the contract, you should also have listed the names and ages of the children the parent will permit to rent games without the adult being present. If you do not have prior written permission from a parent, never permit a game to leave your store in a child's or teenager's custody.

Be sure to keep current with the game market. Keeping up with game requests is good public relations and a way to assure renewal of your customers. Parents will be very receptive to renting a new game for a few days to make certain it's one their children will want to own rather than spending $40 or more only to learn the fascination wears off quickly.

In the beginning it is not necessary to provide carry-out bags for the games. Cartridges are easily carried and the customer usually goes out playing with an electronic game. Later, when your profits allow, you can consider bagging your rentals. Then it's a good idea to use a vinyl type bag with your logo on it. It serves two purposes: The bags are reusable and it's good advertising wherever the bag appears.

You must advertise your new business. A grand opening with balloons and a clown is a wonderful idea. Because Rent-A-Game is a new concept, you might be able to get free advertising by encouraging your local newspaper to run a feature on your store or cover your opening. Also, flyers distributed by bulk mail in your locale will get the word out. And don't forget newspaper ads. They cost, but they'll be well worth the price.

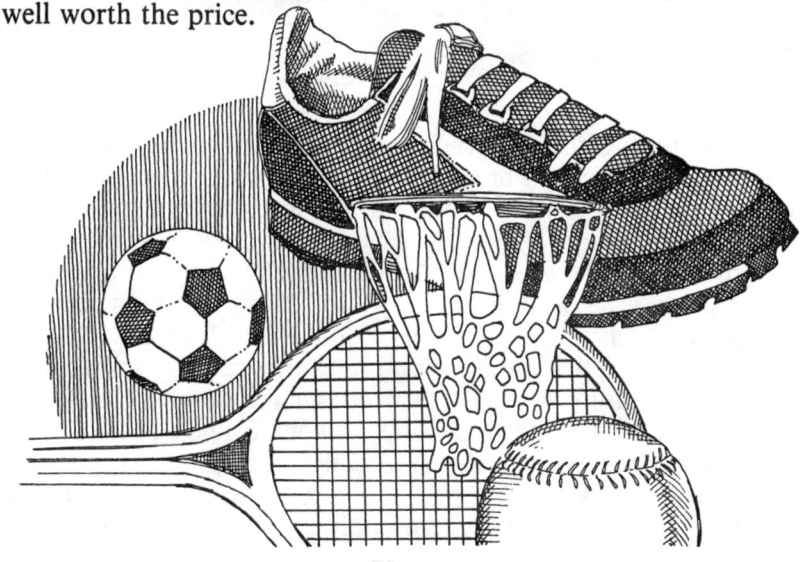

Rent-A-Game can include any type of game that is not vulnerable to easy breakage or loss of pieces. Your inventory can be as large as your imagination. But stay away from items which fall into the "toy" category—those which contain many pieces and require special packaging or show wear quickly, such as dolls and doll clothing, stuffed animals and games such as Monopoly and Chutes and Ladders.

Sports equipment and sporting games can also add to your profits. Businesses and organizations will rent bats, balls and catcher's equipment; soccer, basketball and football gear, and badminton and horseshoe games for their yearly outings. Ping Pong tables and pool tables are also productive rental items for home parties, especially for the teenage set.

Many of these items will not be conducive to your inventory and control card system. You can identify these items with assigned numbers engraved on each item and a separate card file for these rentals. Your local police department will loan you an engraving tool for this purpose or you can purchase one for a minimum amount of money.

If you do extend your inventory to include other types of games and sports equipment, stay within a price range that will permit you to maintain your $3.00 plus $1.00 additional day rental fee. When you're on more stable ground, you can experiment with variably priced items and rental fees. In the beginning keep it as simple as possible.

Give your customers good, friendly service and your renewals should run at least as high as 80 percent. With a well supplied, up-to-date inventory, you could even experience close to a 100 percent renewal. The more renewals, the more cash coming into your business.

Electronic games and cartridges have a long lifespan. You shouldn't have to replace your stock because of wear more often than once a year.

If you continue to maintain a low overhead and keep pouring your profits back into your business in the form of inventory, you can expect your membership roll to reach as high as 1,000 customers. That's $25,000 in membership fees alone. With a 90 percent rental and an inventory of over 1,000 items, you can expect to increase your business' income to:

$ 8,100 per week
$ 32,400 per month
$388,800 per year

That's one store. Imagine if you had two stores, or three, or even a chain of 12. Remember, YOU'RE A FIRST WITH THIS IDEA. The sky's the limit!

CHAPTER NINE

HOW TO START A "BARGAIN BUSINESS"
AND MAKE OVER $390,000 THE FIRST YEAR

Everybody loves a bargain. People will drive miles out of their way to get a bargain even when the extra mileage eats up their savings. They'll talk about their bargain, show it off and even take their friends to get one just like it. If it's an honest-to-goodness bargain, it's irresistible.

Successful entrepreneurs have known this fact for years. Many have become millionaires building their businesses around this concept. It's a concept that doesn't rely on a good economy to succeed. If anything, it pulls more profit when money is tight than when times are easy and the money flows. Satisfying the insatiable urge of the bargain hunter is a sure-fire way for a knowledgeable entrepreneur to make a fortune.

Women's discount clothing stores are all over the country, and are proof that there's big money is selling clothes at bargain prices. In recent years chains of eight and ten stores have blossomed from a single store in only a few years. It's rare to find a large shopping mall that doesn't boast at least one discount women's clothing store. Even the more elegant malls are receptive to bargain clothing stores if they fit into the image of the mall. Shopping mall owners were one of the first to discover that no store can pull in customers like a good quality discount women's clothing store.

Middle class malls also welcome these bargain hunter's delights. Often one good discount store will triple the traffic in the center. Small malls with less restrictive demands as to design and presentation often rely on the women's discount clothing store to keep the other stores afloat.

Discount malls housing only stores carrying discounted merchandise have sprouted up all over the country. Their parking lots are full. Many customers make the discount mall their first stop on any shopping expedition. They brag that they only go elsewhere when the discount mall fails to have the exact item they need at that precise moment. That's a rarity. Some of the best-dressed women admit that they never purchase anything that isn't bought in a discount store or either marked down at least 30 percent in a regular clothing or department store.

A good discount store doesn't have to be associated with a shopping mall or center. Some sit out in the middle of nowhere and attract scores of customers every day. The lack of frills and decoration doesn't faze the serious bargain hunter. It appears that anyone opening a discount women's clothing store can't fail to be a success.

Unfortunately this isn't true. But it could be. There isn't a single good reason why a women's discount clothing store should fail to make lots of money for its owner. The problem lies not in the eagerness of the entrepreneur or his dedicated effort. The problem lies in his thinking. The sure road to minimal profits in this venture is to establish an economic balance based on cheap merchandise and maximum markup.

There are plenty of cheap women's discount stores operating on a shoestring and just managing to stay in business. They offer imports and closeouts for low prices. In these stores the customer gets exactly what he pays for. A $3.00 pair of shorts is a $3.00 pair of shorts. On occasion the pair of shorts may be worth $5.00. Usually in these stores a bargain is not a bargain just because it's been presented as one. Often the merchandise is flawed and the workmanship poor. You won't find a well-dressed, fashion-conscious woman shopping this type of discount clothing store.

The successful owner of a discount women's clothing store takes a different approach. He thinks quality merchandise at high volume. The success formula is simple. The more garments you sell, the more money you automatically make. The more you sell, the more you can afford to operate at a lower markup. By selling manufacturer's quality overruns, closeouts and cancellations which you can purchase for a mere pittance you can keep the cost of your inventory at a minimum. The lower the cost of your inventory, the lower your markup can be. In fact, truly high volume can enable you to price all your merchandise at $10.00 or less.

Imagine selling a $50 dress for $10. Imagine your customer's reaction when she discovers a pair of $40 wool pants for $10. How many customers will rush to your store to buy a $70 silk blouse for $10? Keep thinking volume in this context and putting it into action and you'll find yourself grossing millions of dollars almost before you know it.

A quick turnover of your inventory is vital. Regular women's clothing stores turn their inventory a maximum of six times a year. To make the big bucks and be successful, you must turn your inventory a minimum of every four weeks. That's twelve times a year. And if you can keep your merchandise moving and turn it more often, say even fourteen or sixteen times a year, you'll reap more profits than you believed possible.

Give your customers a true bargain and your store will be filled not only with the fashion-conscious individual who knows quality, but with every woman who shops and is smart enough not to spend one more cent than she has to on her wardrobe or the wardrobe of her family.

Good quality merchandise is readily available at amazingly low cost. You just have to know where to look.

Clothing manufacturers and distributors are located throughout the country. There are many in the New York City area, Dallas, Houston, Chicago, and in many California cities. You must visit these manufacturers. Select those closest to you and then do your homework.

Get a copy of those cities' Yellow Pages and call the manufacturers and distributors listed. Go for quality brand names that you and your customers know. Find out when these managers receive buyers. Plan an itinerary that will take you to every manufacturer and distributor that can possibly sell to you. Projecting your most professional image, pay them all a visit.

Tell the managers that you are opening a women's quality discount clothing store and that your selling concept will be based on volume and rapid turnover. This means you will be selling in-season garments. When the department stores and regular clothing stores are showing winter suits, coats and dresses in July, your store will still be selling cotton sundresses and lightweight slacks, shorts, skirts and tops—items women will still need and will be unable to buy elsewhere.

The manufacturer will immediately understand that he now has a market for all the out-of-season merchandise which is now sitting in his warehouse unsold, taking up costly space. He would like very much to be rid of it. In fact, so much so that he will be willing to sell it at a very low price. Of course, the larger quantity you buy, the more eager he will be to sell the merchandise at an even lower price. Rid him of all this unwanted stock and he'll practically give the merchandise to you.

Much of this merchandise is the result of overruns. This is perfectly fine quality merchandise but there was just too much of it for it all to be sold during that particular merchandising season. Cancellations account for much of it, too. Buyers over-order and stores do go out of business. Perfectly beautiful and expensive merchandise remains unsold through no fault of its own.

Don't automatically cross off manufacturers of imported merchandise. You can find fine quality and get good pricing from reputable importers, especially those manufacturers which deal in higher class clothing. Just stay away from the "cheapies." Remember, you're running a class act and whenever you slip beneath this level you'll not only lose your customers but be off the track that is the key to making you a wealthy retailer.

Normally manufacturers aren't interested in talking to the little man who has only one store. They're even less inclined to talk to the man who hasn't even opened a store. However, you can convince him that you're worth talking to. Prepare an impressive presentation that will convince him that even if you can't buy in the volume he prefers today, a few months down the road you will be able to and within a couple of years your goal is to own several stores and eventually a chain of ten or twelve stores. This will certainly get his attention.

Present him with a folder showing your expenditures versus your projected gross. Don't stop at a one-year presentation. It's worth the additional time and effort to be able to show him a projected statement for the next year, three years and even five years. Let him know that he's talking to a man who's competent, optimistic and determined. A guy who's on his way to doing business in a big way.

A solid, well prepared presentation will not only get you the merchandise you need to open your first store, but you'll probably even talk him into giving you the volume pricing you need to open a store where you can price every piece of merchandise at $10 or less.

Impress the manufacturer with your concern for quality. Inspect his merchandise carefully. Make him aware that you're only interested in clothing that is made of quality fabric and fine workmanship. Don't buy a single garment that isn't worth far more than the price tag you're going to attach to it. The more selective you are, the better value your customers will receive and the better reputation you'll have with the manufacturers as a consumer who is quality conscious, selective and concerned about his customers.

Although it will cost you additional money, always do your buying in person. You can't afford surprise shipments in this business and they can happen from even the finest manufacturers. What you are seeking is quality far superior to any your customers will find at your competition and for far less money.

Build your contacts in the garment industry and maintain them. Keep in touch each time you're in the area. Always be business-like, well mannered and honest. Let them know that you're a reputable businessman. It will gain you much in the long run. First, manufacturers will be more eager to give you the lowest possible pricing. They'll also remember you and when they have merchandise they know will interest you, they'll call you. In time, the two of you may even grow and develop enough trust that you can have occasional orders shipped to you without first making a trip and personally inspecting the merchandise.

You'll also find yourself in the position to receive credit sooner. In the beginning, you will probably have to pay COD or by credit card for every item you order. As your reliability and credibility is proven, the manufacturer who personally knows and respects you will be quicker to permit you to purchase on credit.

In most cases, your merchandise will be shipped parcel post. But as you deal in greater quantities, it will have to be shipped by truck. Use trucking firms that are the shortest point between the manufacturer and your store. Don't pay for extra miles. Trucking companies will furnish you with rate sheets upon request.

Your store and its appearance are also of major importance to your success. First, you want to establish and maintain the image of a quality and fashion-conscious retailer. Your store must be pleasant looking and clean. Avoid anything that is old or looks cheap, including light fixtures, racks and hangers. Keep your decorating simple and in good taste. Carpeting on the floor and lots of displays are a plus. Put together and accessorize outfits. This can be as simple as a blouse on a hangar with a sweater over it, a scarf at the neck and a belt. This not only encourages the customer to buy additional pieces of merchandise but makes your store look more fashion conscious.

Go for a prime location. A top class mall is your best bet if your ultimate goal is million-dollar status. Give the mall owners the same presentation you gave the manufacturers. Convince them that they too are going to be doing business with a winner. The higher class your location, the higher class bargain hunter you'll attract and the more money they'll have to spend and the more money you'll make. An artist's concept and design of your store will convince the mall owner that a $10 clothing store can look every bit as classy as a major department store.

It may seem like a minor point, but make certain that your sales personnel make an excellent appearance. Attractive, well dressed personnel who are articulate and service-oriented are a must. They not only are a welcome surprise to the shopper in a discount store, but they can help the customer put together complete outfits and wardrobes, just like in the best clothing stores. Again, this makes more money for you.

You can save on overhead in your dressing rooms. Customers don't seem to care about privacy when they're getting genuine bargains. It's been proven that community dressing rooms are not a deterrent to the bargain shopper. You can also save on a security system. Surprisingly, shoplifting is low in this type of store and when you do lose a few garments you haven't lost a tremendous amount of money. After your grand opening, you won't need an advertising budget, either. Repeat customers and word of mouth will keep yur store full of bargain buyers.

The most important element in your store design is getting the most money out of every square foot of space. Let's say your store contains 1200 square feet. Use every possible inch that you can to display your inventory. When your customer walks into your store, you want to amaze her with a vast array of choices. If you can carry at least 8000 items and have every one of them out on display or on shelving or racks. Bargain hunters don't mind narrow aisles or having to wind their way through a maze of racks. The more square footage you use profitably, the higher your return per square foot.

Maintain a professional high-class attitude in your store. Have your signs professionally printed and package your sales in vinyl bags with your logo printed on them. Also, accept checks and credit cards. Your customers will view this as a courtesy and another sign of class. But you must insist on no returns or refunds. A sign on the wall over your cash register will emphasize this policy. Your sale personnel should also remind the customer of this before she pays for the merchandise. If you make certain your customers understand this policy before they buy, it won't be a problem.

To make money with a $10 women's discount clothing store, you'll have to invest money. This is not an operation you can start on a mere shoestring. But it is an operation that will quickly turn an enormous profit and make a quick return on your investment.

First, you must have the capital to purchase your inventory. That will amount to 3/4 of your initial investment in garments costing $3 and $4 each. Buy a minimum of 5000 garments to start with and with as much variety as possible. That will amount to $17,500. One-quarter of your investment will be required to open and furnish your facility and that amounts to $4,375. Your minimum initial investment will be $21,875.

Now, what kind of income can you expect to make? If you sell 5000 garments every four weeks at a $6.50 markup, maintaining your $10 ceiling on price, you will make $32,500 per month. That's $390,000 per year. Your operating budget will probably run 30 percent and amount to $117,000. You will then have netted $273,000 your first year and on only one store!

If you purchase 10,000 garments every four weeks, your figures will be even more impressive using the above calculating method:

$780,000 gross per year
$234,000 operating budget

$546,000 net profit per year for one store.

As you can see, it certainly won't take you long to have the capital to open a second, third or even fourth store. A chain of twelve is well within your possibility. And it certainly won't take you long to watch your net figures climb into the million-dollar bracket. It does take a little more effort than many of the new ideas being offered, but it's a good, solid business operation and one that can be learned quickly and controlled by a minimum of administrative personnel, even when your few stores grow into a lengthy chain. And the biggest problem you'll encounter in your $10 discount women's clothing store is opening enough stores to satisfy all the people who will want one in their area.

**Women's Sportswear
Wholesalers & Manufacturers**

Abbey Road Ltd.
1407 Broadway
New York, NY

B&F Mfg. Ltd.
1411 Broadway
New York, NY

Barclay Square Inc.
1400 Broadway
New York, NY

Best of Friends
112 W. 34th
New York, NY

Brook House
232 Madison Avenue
New York, NY

Casey Mfg. Inc.
132 W. 36th
New York, NY

Cross Roads Mfg. Inc.
340 W. 39th
New York, NY

Daniel Laurent Ltd.
589 8th Avenue
New York, NY

Deer Variety Fashions
31 Orchard
New York, NY

Eccobay Sportswear Inc.
1431 Broadway
New York, NY

Fire Islander Woman
1407 Broadway
New York, NY

G&C Creations Inc.
53 Orchard
New York, NY

Gailord Classics Inc.
1407 Broadway
New York, NY

Gina Originals Inc.
1359 Broadway
New York, NY

Harbour Road Inc.
1411 Broadway
New York, NY

Haymaker Sports Inc.
498 7th Avenue
New York, NY

Hi-Lite Sport & Knitwear Corp.
328 Grand
New York, NY

Lady Devon
1411 Broadway
New York, NY

Lido Sportswear
135 W. 50th
New York, NY

Mel Mortman Inc.
525 7th Avenue
New York, NY

**Women's Skirts
Wholesalers & Manufacturers**

Capriccio International Inc.
525 7th Avenue
New York, NY

Carlton Garment Co.
692 Broadway
New York, NY

Chic Togs Fashions
470 7th Avenue
New York, NY

D&M Sportswear Mfg. Co.
29 Allen
New York, NY

Daisy Sportswear Inc.
212 W. 35th
New York, NY

Hazen Sportswear Co.
462 7th Avenue
New York, NY

Ina Sportswear
20 W. 20th
New York, NY

Jonbarry Originials Inc.
525 7th Avenue
New York, NY

Klassiks Ltd.
830 W. 34th
New York, NY

Lady Arrow
1407 Broadway
New York, NY

**Women's Apparel
Contract Manufacturers**
A&G Sportswear
9309 S. Vermont Ave.
Los Angeles, CA

Anthony's of California
1940 E. 65th
Los Angeles, CA

B&M Sportswear
620 S. Main
Los Angeles, CA

California Visionz
746 S. Los Angeles St.
Los Angeles, CA

Chrissy Lyn Fashions
4327 Brooklyn Ave.
Los Angeles, CA

De La Rosa Fashions
930 S. Broadway
Los Angeles, CA

Edel of California
121 E. 6th
Los Angeles, CA

Grand Prix Sewing Co.
315 E. 8th
Los Angeles, CA

Honeybee
5401 Cudahy Ave.
Maywood, CA

J&R Factory
7810 Seville Ave.
Huntingdon Park, CA

**Women's Coats & Suits
Wholesalers & Manufacturers**
California Affair
2240 S. Main
Los Angeles, CA

Charles Mr. of California
8031 W. Sunset Blvd.
Los Angeles, CA

Deanna Dee
860 S. Los Angeles St.
Los Angeles, CA

Dumas of California
932 S. Hill
Los Angeles, CA

Jet Set of California
850 S. Broadway
Los Angeles, CA

Jordache Blazers & Suits
116 E. 9th
Los Angeles, CA

Mayfair Coat & Suit Co.
217 E. 8th
Los Angeles, CA

Strauss Ernst Inc.
714 S. Los Angeles St.
Los Angeles, CA

Suncraft Coats
834 S. Broadway
Los Angeles, CA

Walter Louis Co. Inc.
425 E. Pico Blvd.
Los Angeles, CA

Women's Accessories Wholesalers

Accessories du Jour
1206 Maple Ave.
Los Angeles, CA

Accessories International
1011 E. 8th
Los Angeles, CA

Alden Howard Design Studios
920 S. Broadway
Los Angeles, CA

Avion International Inc.
110 E. 9th
Los Angeles, CA

Carole Inc.
110 E. 9th
Los Angeles, CA

Dalon Hosiery
110 E. 9th
Los Angeles, CA

Fels Co.
212 W. Olympic Blvd.
Los Angeles, CA

Glensder Corp.
110 E. 9th
Los Angeles, CA

Les Centurions Corp.
3671 S. Broadway
Los Angeles, CA

Saint Raymond
1015 E. 14th
Los Angeles, CA

CHAPTER TEN

$25,000 IN SIX WEEKS IS HARD TO BEAT!

Make $25,000 for only six week's work and do nothing the rest of the year?

Sound too good to be true? Well, it isn't. Not only can you do it, but it's easy. You don't have to learn anything extremely complicated, develop a technical skill or forcefully sell any product. You simply do something you've already done many times before—only this time you get paid big money for doing it.

All of us are familiar with the yearly Christmas hassle of getting all our presents bought and wrapped. Far too often the buying is the easy part. After we have our gift in hand, we usually must elbow our way to a boxing area where we get to wait in line with many other people. During the holiday season this wait can stretch to half an hour and even longer. Then when we finally get to the head of the line, we must show a sales slip, which is usually in the wrong bag and difficult to find, before the department store clerk will give us a box for our gift. Unfortunately this is a procedure which must be repeated each time we purchase a gift that needs a box.

As difficult as it is to get a simple gift box in a department store, in many small shops—even in the finest malls—it's an impossibility. Many stores just don't want to be bothered with the time-consuming courtesy and expense of providing boxes for their customers.

These reasons are the same ones that motivate department stores to provide a separate area where you must go to collect your gift box. During the holiday season many people are just too tired to walk to these out-of-the-way places. Instead they just leave the store frustrated and without the box or boxes. This, of course, saves the store money on the boxes and the personnel necessary to provide this service.

But even if you do stand in line and get your box, you still aren't done with your gift package. You either have to gift wrap it yourself or have it gift wrapped. Doing it yourself is not something many people enjoy doing unless they're getting paid for it. You also have to purchase the white tissue for the inside of your gift box, wrapping paper, cellophane tape and ribbon. At retail prices all of these items are expensive. To purchase the proper wrapping essentials to gift wrap a standard size box, 11x11x2 inches, for a shirt or sweater will usually cost you $3.00 or more. That isn't counting the cost of the box if you have to pay for it. So you've invested at least $3.00 and maybe, just maybe, you'll have enough paper left over to wrap one more very tiny present. And you still have to do the wrapping yourself. If you don't like to wrap presents, the worst part is still ahead of you. That's why Christmas is such a chore for so many. Few people enjoy gift wrapping.

That's very good news for the part-time entrepreneur. It's amazing how quickly you can learn to love gift wrapping for only six weeks each year when it means $25,000 in your Christmas stocking. And you have to admit how easy it really it. You simply cover the box with a piece of paper cut to fit with a slight overlap on each end of the box. Place a piece of tape in the center back to connect the paper ends, diagonally fold the flaps at each end, making sure they're neat and tight, fold them over and tape each flap to the back of the package. You've got a wrapped package in almost the same length of time it takes Santa to zoom up the chimney. It's even easier to wind ribbon around the box once, twice will add to your cost, and tie it. Big, fancy bows are no problem. Bow-making gadgets are available from wholesalers and in variety stores and are inexpensive. They'll whip up professional looking bows for you in a matter of seconds. Attach the bow to the package and in less than ten minutes you've wrapped a package your customer will be delighted to pay for. In addition, you've spared him a long waiting period, if any waiting period at all, and you've provided him with a box and gift wrapping all in one place. You're also doing it all at competitive pricing with the department stores. Best of all for you, you'll be making a 169 percent markup on every package you and your employees wrap!

Now that you're eager to begin, where do you start? A good location is a large mall containing as many as 90 stores. Here you can expect to wrap at peak quantity and at a continual pace. There is one drawback in locating your temporary mall wrapping booth in a shopping center of this size. The average rental fee will be $250 to $350 per week. This will add to your overhead but it will be covered by the additional packages you will wrap in a mall of this size. However, these large malls will have a large list of restrictions which will govern your business. Make certain that these restrictions will not limit your income or increase your initial investment or expenditures. Remember, you're not renting a store in the mall, only a small area space within the mall walkway.

A small mall or discount mall is also a good bet. One advantage to locating in these malls is that you won't be competing with the large department stores which offer gift-wrapping departments. Usually the stores located in these centers offer no boxing or gift wrapping. You'll have the market all to yourself. These centers also will cost you much less in rental. Fees for a mall area booth here can run $150 to as little as $50 per week.

Some of these malls may even rent you space on a percentage deal. This means you won't have to pay your first week's rental in advance. Your percentage will be due the end of each week. Be sure you understand the percentage you'll be paying. Unless it's very low you could end up paying more than a flat rental. Of course, you want your rental space in the mall to cost you as little as possible.

A medium size mall of 60 to 75 stores is your best bet. You'll benefit from the heavy traffic flow, there will be a large enough number of stores to provide you with the quantity of wrapping you'll need to make your $25,000 goal, and the competition from the smaller size department stores in these malls will make your wrapping, pricing and quick service obviously a much better deal. In addition, the rental average for temporary mall space in this size center is only $100 per week and there are very few restrictions placed on your business.

No matter where you choose to establish your holiday gift wrapping business, you will have to supply your own booth. There are display manufacturers who furnish booths listed in the Yellow Pages of telephone books in the major cities. Tent and awning manufacturers, as well as some party caterers, can also supply appropriate size booths with fancy, eye-catching canopies. Rental and installation of these booths will cost you anywhere from $200 to $500, plus an additional rental charge per week. And this will cover only the basic booth.

It is much simpler and more economical for you to provide your own booth. In addition, next year when you want to set up your six-weeks gift wrapping service again, your booth won't cost you a cent. A do-it-yourself booth will be a one-time expense.

Your biggest booth expense will be your counter area. Six 72x30 sturdy, office-style folding tables will provide you with a U-shaped three-sided booth measuring 12 feet on each side.

Happy Holidays

These six tables should cost you less than $250 from a used office wholesaler. A simple, sturdy plywood sheet will serve as the backside of your booth with a walk-around area at its edges. If you're even the least bit handy with hammer and nails, you can construct simple easel-style braces to hold the booth back securely and safely in place. This makes your booth completely portable and easily transported in either a station wagon or van. The cost is less than $60.00.

Now all you need is a cash register and a stand to put it on. A large, strong second-hand table will run you around $30. A reconditioned, used cash register will fulfill your needs and cost only $100 from a wholesale cash register supplier.

Decorate your booth with paint and fabric. Paint your backboard a cheerful Christmas red and attach hooks at random across the upper half. These hooks can be purchased cheaply at any hardware store. On the bottom half of your backboard attach roller rods with wide, deep brackets to hold your rolls of wrapping paper and ribbon. Purchase inexpensive red fabric to thumbtack or staple to the outside of your tables so that it will hang from the outside top of the table to the floor. This will give you hidden storage area beneath the tables for your boxes and extra rolls of wrapping paper. Completing your booth in this efficient and colorful manner should cost you no more than $150.

Wrap at least six different style packages as displays. Attach them to the hooks on your backboard. Your customers can then see the quality and beauty of your work and select the style wrapping and paper which most appeals to them.

You will now have an attractive, stylish gift wrapping booth which measures 12 feet square, is situated within the mall walkway area, and which will easily attract the attention of your customers. It will also meet most discriminating codes governing shopping malls. The cost: $600 maximum.

Inventory is your next step. Check the Yellow Pages of your local telephone book for inventory supply houses carrying the materials you will need. If you deal with a supplier close to your home base, you'll be able to pick up your merchandise and save expensive delivery and transportation charges. Some wholesalers will carry everything you need: boxes, white tissue paper, wrapping paper, ribbon, cellophane tape, bow makers. By buying all your supplies from one wholesaler, you should get a better price break than shopping several different wholesalers. Look under "Boxes" in your Yellow Pages.

So how much inventory should you purchase? The six weeks prior to Christmas are the biggest shopping weeks of the year. Each day thousands of shoppers pass through a medium size mall and most buy several gifts each. You will certainly not lack for customers. It will be wise of you to stay open the same hours as the stores in the mall. For these six weeks the hours are usually nine in the morning until ten at night. You will want to keep five part-timers manning your booth at all times to provide the quick service holiday shoppers are seeking. This means you will need seven employees with staggered hours, plus yourself, to keep your booth functioning on a full-time basis. Each part-timer will earn $3.85 per hour and it should take her no longer than ten minutes to wrap a package and complete the business transaction of payment. That's six packages per employee per hour, or a minimum of 30 gifts wrapped per hour, or 330 gifts wrapped per day. Wrapping 2,310 packages per 7-day week over a six week period means your inventory must be sufficient to wrap at least 13,860 packages during your temporary business venture.

Boxes come in all sizes, shapes and colors. You will need a variety of sizes and you should purchase in volume for the best price, even if the amount slightly exceeds your needs. A standard 11x11x2 two-piece gift box suitable for a blouse, sweater and many other types of gifts will cost you 22 cents per box wholesale. Purchasing a variety of 15,000 boxes will amount to $3,300.00. For a slightly higher price the wholesaler will offer a wide variety of boxes in colors and different styles but this will be a package deal, so be sure you'll be able to use all the various sizes and shapes if you consider this type of selection.

Pennington's Gift Wrapping

Perhaps Make an Advertisement As Shown Above.

White tissue paper for lining the interior of your boxes adds to your expense but it's a must for a first-class operation. 15,000 sheets will cost you $248.70. Your customers will expect them and they're a plus to a professionally wrapped package.

Paper curling ribbon is the least expensive ribbon, only $3.00 per 250 yards, but it will cheapen your wrapping quality. Use sasheen ribbon. It costs much more but wraps a more beautiful package and makes a lovely bow. Each package will require approximately two yards of ribbon for both the wrapping and the bow so you'll need 120 rolls of ribbon in 250-yard spools at $10.00 per spool. This amounts to $1,200.00.

Wrapping paper comes in a wide selection of design, quality and price. Buying wholesale will enable you to get a good selection of a fair quality paper at $75.00 per 833-foot roll measuring 24 inches wide. It will take an average of one foot of 24-inch wide paper to wrap each present. You will get 833 gifts wrapped out of each roll. Eighteen rolls will provide you with the paper to wrap 14,994 gifts. This will cost you $1,350.00. An ample amount to cover the various size gifts you will be wrapping.

Your additional expenditures and entire inventory for the six weeks of your wrapping business will amount to the following:

Boxes (15,000 11x11x2)	$3,300.00
Paper (18 rolls wrap 14,994 gifts)	$1,350.00
Tissue (15,000 sheets)	$ 248.70
Ribbon (120 spools for 15,000 gifts)	$1,200.00
Cellophane tape, Bow makers, Scissors, etc.	$ 150.00
Total	$6,248.70

★★

Now add the $600 expense for your booth and your investment will amount to $6,848.70. If this $6,848.70 inventory expenditure is beyond your means at this time, you can easily reduce it to a <u>fourth</u> or approximately $1,500.00. Just simply order a fourth the inventory you'll need for six weeks. You'll be dealing with a local wholesaler who will have these items in stock through the holiday season. When your inventory begins to run low, you will have accumulated the cash to go back to your supplier and pick up the remaining inventory necessary to carry you through your next two weeks.

How much should you charge per package? Your per-piece expenditures and inventory break down as follows:

Boxes	$ .22 each
Paper	$ .09 each
Tissue	$ .02 each
Ribbon	$ .08 each
Cellophane tape, bow makers, scissors, etc.	$ .01 min.
Total	$ .42 each package

But you must also include your labor expense per package. With seven part-time employees working staggered hours, five on at all times, your labor costs will amount to $211.75 per day. Wrapping 330 packages a day makes your labor charge per package $ .64. Added to your expenditures and inventory charge of $ .42 brings your total cost per package to $1.06.

Your competition will charge between $2.85 and $3.00 per wrapped gift. Price your gift wrapping fee at $2.85. You'll be making $1.79 per each package you and your employees wrap. That amounts to an impressive 169 percent markup!

$ 590.70 per day
$ 4,134.90 per week
$24,809.40 for your six weeks in business.
That's nearly $25,000!

One of the nicest things about your temporary gift wrapping business is the extremely low overhead. You needn't have your employees' first week salary in your initial investment. That expense will be accumulated as each package is wrapped and be ready for you to pay them at the end of your first week in business.

Remember, next year your net profit will be even greater because you'll have your portable booth paid for and ready to go. Plus, if you want to make even more quick money during the year, you might consider setting up your temporary gift wrapping booth for Valentine's Day, Easter, and the May and June wedding and graduation gift rush. You may just be able to double your income into a $50,000 part-time business.

CHAPTER ELEVEN

SIT AT HOME — AND EARN $100,000 ANNUALLY!

If you are the sit-at-home thinker-type then this business is exactly what the doctor ordered. Have you ever wondered where all those "BRIGHT INTERESTING" local radio and TV commercials came from? Well stop wondering! Most of them come from free lance advertising agencies, just like the one I am going to show you how to open and put into operation as early as next week.

This is a business you can start with as little as $25 and earn as much as $100,000 or more the first year without ever leaving your home. (That's right, it is not a misprint. I said start with $25 and earn up to $100,000 the first year. Stay with me and I'll show you how!)

Believe it or not, this business is as easy as writing to your sweetheart. All there is to know about writing commercials for retailers and other local advertisers is in this chapter.

Please read it slowly.
Let's Begin!
You're really not expected, at this time, to have a lot of knowledge about specific businesses, such as womansclothing stores, retail tire stores, stereo systems, draperies, carpets, restaurants, motels, all the businesses that advertise on local TV and radio. If you do happen to know something about a particular kind of business, fine. Use what you know. But it's actually an advantage not to know too much. You're less likely to fall into the trap of using terms the general public won't understand.

There are other reasons why retail and local commercials are good to get started on and maybe specialize in permanently. One is, there are so many of them, and—unlike much advertising for packaged goods that runs unchanged for years—retail and local advertising changes pretty often, so there's lots of writing to be done. Even if all you're doing is changing your basic commercial from VALENTINE'S DAY SALE to EASTER SALE to MOTHER'S DAY SALE, somebody has to get paid for doing the rewrite, and it might as well be you.

Another thing: while the big national products have advertising agencies with highly experienced writers turning out commercials the way McDonald's makes hamburgers, many local advertisers do not, and writing commercials is a painful process for them. If they have big advertising departments producing newspaper ads for them, they're in even worse shape. The cliches which readers accept in newspaper ads, the third person style (instead of the "you" second person style of good broadcast writing and ordinary conversation) comes out stilted and phony over the air. Rarely can somebody in a newspaper-oriented advertising department break these writing habits of a lifetime. So the advertiser goes outside for help. To you, if he knows you're ready to go to work, if you've sent him a couple of commercials for style. Or to a radio or TV station, who may also turn to you—if you have let them know you are available, and have written some sample commercials for them— because generally they're not staffed to write commercials.

If advertisers and stations come to rely on you to write commercials for them, you are in effect an advertising agency, and you may want to make it legal. The good news is you get 15% commission on the time cost. Even a small advertiser, spending, let's say, $1,000 a week, will bring you $150 a week income as long as the commercial runs. It's not uncommon for a single commercial—100 words or so on a single sheet of paper, taking maybe half an hour at the most to write—to earn its author $50,000 or more over a couple of years. *THATS JUST ONE COMMERCIAL!*

This is not a history of broadcasting, or a textbook that you must study before you begin writing commercials. We're going to start out as if you were already working—freelance—for a radio or TV station or advertising agency. I'll give you an assignment just the way you would get it on the job, and you write the commercial.

So grab some blank paper and a pen or pencil or a typewriter and let's write some commercials!

Everybody hates car dealer commercials. Why? because there are so many of them on the air, and most of them are terrible. From your point of view, that's good, because you'll never be out of work if you can write car dealer commercials, no matter how bad they are. And if you write good ones you can make lots of money.

LOOK AT EXAMPLE #1 — DATSUN DEALER CLASSIFIED AD.

The sales manager of the radio station says to you, "We'd like to sell this guy some time. See what you can come up with in the way of a commercial."

First step, see if this ad can be easily adapted to a commercial without making many changes. There are some advantages to doing this if you can. The dealer has already approved this copy for his classified ad. In fact, he may have written it himself and thinks it's wonderful.

So try it aloud. Maybe it's pretty close to an acceptable commercial as it is, with a few changes.

Take a minute and do this right now.

* * * *

Hopeless, right? A jumble of unrelated statements, starting with meaningless self-praise (who cares if they're #1? #1 in what, anyway? profit?) jumping to store hours, to parts and service, back to cars, on to a weak claim about CREDIT ("we will try to arrange"—they make it sound hopeless!) and finally, their address and phone number.

LET'S MAKE A SILK PURSE OUT OF THIS SOW'S EAR

Well, let's try to fatten our own purse, anyway. First, take a sheet of paper and list the elements in this ad.

You should have eight elements: (1) claim of #1, (2) hours, (3) parts and service, (4) "You will never know....", (5) over 75 Z's, (6) over 400 cars for sale, (7) credit, (8) address.

Now see what you can do by juggling these elements around and eliminating what isn't essential for each commercial. Actually, there are several fair commercials buried in this hodgepodge. Enough for not just one commercial, but for a campaign—a series of commercials—which should make the sales manager of the station very happy with you.

For a start, take YOU WILL NEVER KNOW....as your theme, and use whatever other elements seem to support that proposition.

For exercise, try writing a commercial that starts out YOU WILL NEVER KNOW and uses only elements (1) #1, (2) hours, and (8) address. Do it in roughest form. Try not to take more than 15 minutes.

Finished? You probably have something like this:
You will never know if you got the best deal on a new Datsun unless you check with the Number One Dealer—Universal City Datsun. That's why Universal City Datsun is open extra hours—until 10 every night, including Saturday and Sunday—so you can check, compare the price, compare the trade-in allowance you get from Universal City Datsun with the best offer you've had from any other Datsun dealer anywhere. You could save a lot of money. It's certainly worth taking the time to check with the Number One Datsun dealer before you make a deal. It's easy to get to Universal Datsun. Take the Hollywood Freeway to Lankershim-Universal City Off-ramp in North Hollywood: Turn left and you're there. Universal Datsun.

That isn't much of a commercial, but it's no worse than most of the car dealer advertising on the air, and lots better than the ad you adapted to create it. Notice that although you used only four elements, you reorganized them to support your main theme: YOU WILL NEVER KNOW UNLESS... You used the theme to make the hours and address important.

So far, you've done nothing but enumerate (the elements), manipulate them and eliminate half of them.

You could do the same thing with elements (2) hours, (6) over 400 for sale, and (8) address and phone. You might do something like this:

Listen to the following important announcement. Universal Datsun will be open until 10 o'clock tonight and every night, Saturday and Sunday included, for a special sale of over 400 Datsuns...

...and so on through the address. I won't take the space to write out sample commercials using all the possible variations, because we have more interesting things to go on to. But you should do this. You might try picking elements almost at random and have fun arranging them in different sequences. You could begin with (8) address, for instance.

Next time you're driving down the Hollywood Freeway, turn off at the Lankershim-Universal City off-ramp.... and continue with... *that's where Universal City Datsun is having a sale of 400 Datsuns...*

...and so on.

Try a few, then come back.

Now take the next step: thumb through the pages of today's paper. Pick out the worst ads you can find and see how easy it is to create salable commercials just by doing these three things: enumerate, manipulate, eliminate. As you do it, practice substituting common ordinary conversational English for the cliches you find in so many ads. Just write the way people talk. Read what you write aloud, as you go along, and change anything that doesn't sound natural, doesn't sound as though you were just talking to a friend.

Take a break now to go through the paper. When you've outlined five commercials, come back and we'll take another step beyond enumerate, manipulate, eliminate.

Don't think we've finished with car commercials. They're too important. You could earn a great living writing nothing but car commercials. You might find it boring, but no more boring than hearing and seeing them all day and all night on radio and TV, and you'd be getting paid, which is more than the audience gets.

In fact, you could probably make your first money today. Knowing nothing more than how to enumerate, manipulate and eliminate, you could pick a car dealer's ad out of the paper, convert it to a radio commercial and pick up your first check as a commercial writer. But you might as well learn a few more tricks of the trade, radio and TV. Then we'll come back to automobile commercials and see if we can make them less boring as well as more effective.

Let's write a TV commercial now. Just for the fun of it, let's pick a classification (a) where there's plenty of money to be made and (b) that a lot of writers already on the payroll (!) of the advertiser or the broadcasting station give up on before they even get started.

Pick a big department store ad, or a supermarket; any big space ad with a lot of items. "Impossible!" someone will say. How are you going to get all those items into a 60-second, let alone a 30-second commercial? Watch and see how easy it is to convert this to TV.

The first ad of any size I saw in today's paper happens to be a 2-page spread for a big drug chain. It illustrates 48 items.

If we wanted to, we could do this easily, using one of the oldest tricks in TV. We'd simply show the ad on TV. Before you write this off as too, too awful to consider, let's see how a clever sales manager of a TV station would use this terrible commercial to get some of this advertiser's money out of newspaper and into TV.

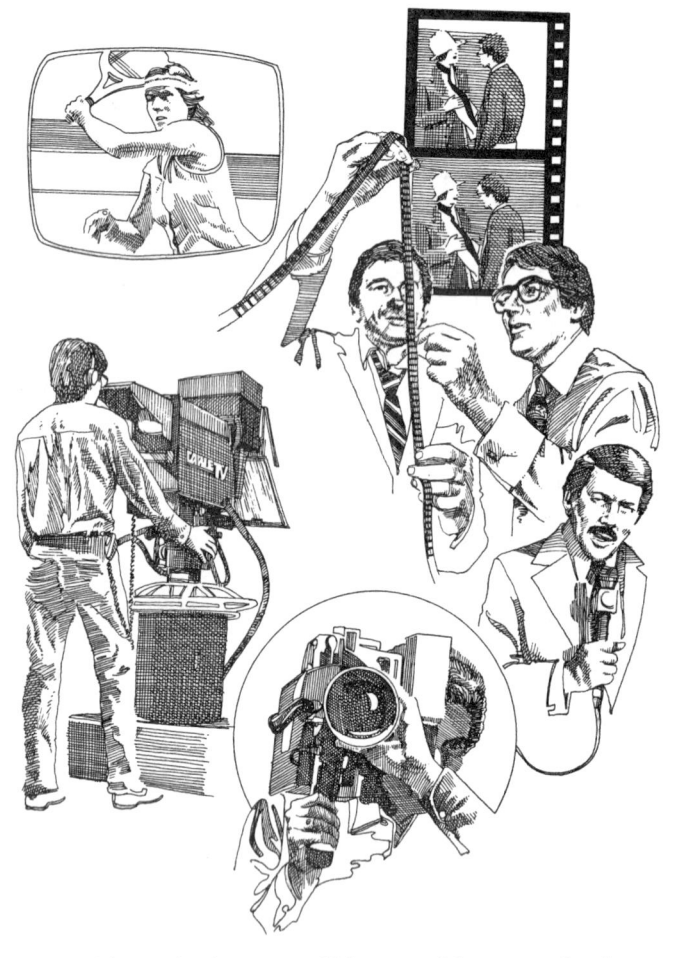

"Your ad in today's paper," he would say to the boss of the drug chain, "cost $10,000."

"Although the newspaper has a circulation of approximately one million, you and I know that only a small percentage of that one million people will actually read any part of your ad. I'd say no more than 20%."

The boss of the drug chain may argue this figure briefly, but probably not. He knows it is probably too high, if anything.

"And you and I know," continues the salesman for TV, "that there is really nothing you can do (that you haven't already done) in the layout of the ad to increase the readership over 20%."

"But by running a few TV spots at a fraction of the cost of your newspaper ad," continues the TV time salesman, warming to his subject, "you can increase the number of readers of your ad, the number of people you're paying $10,000 for. By increasing the number of readers by only 10%, we've actually added 50%, or $5,000, to the value of your newspaper ad."

At that point, he shows the commercial copy, which starts out with the announcer, who is reading the paper, turning to the audience and—with astonishment and delight in her voice (yes, this would probably be a lady announcer) saying:

Did you see this ad in today's paper? Did you see the sale Thrifty Drug is having? Look at this!....

...and so on.

Let's see how this looks in script form, the TV video directions on the left, the audio on the right, standard form. We'll use a few camera directions. The terms are obvious. ANNCR is announcer. CU is closeup. ECU is extreme closeup. MS is medium shot. CAM #1 is camera one. MUSIC FX is music effects. STINGER is a short musical effect, like a trumpet flourish. SIG SLIDE is a slide, a regular 35mm slide, like the ones your camera takes, of the advertiser's signature, or LOGO or SIG, as it is sometimes called.

VIDEO	AUDIO
1 MS over ANNCR'S shoulder; push in for MCU as she turns to CAM #1.	*Did you see the ad on page 18 in today's Times, for the sale Thrifty is having?*
2 Push in for ECU item: digital alarm clock. Dissolve to matching position of actual product at same angle as in ad.	*$10.99 for this digital alarm clock!*
3 Cut to CAM #2; pull back rapidly from matching shot of digital alarm clock to show other merchandise, live, on set simulating store counters, as ANNCR pre-taped walks into scene, along aisle.	*and here's a Shakespeare reel, $9.99; Old Spice Shave Cream, $1.33; color film, $1.09...I could go on and on...sleeping bags, $11.99 ...Don't miss this sale, today and tomorrow.*

4 Full screen SIG slide	*MUSIC FX* *only at Thrifty Drug Stores.*

In this simple, almost primitive commercial, we have—technically, in the set simulated a store interior, with merchandise we scan, price tags and all, as we follow the announcer in her short stroll down the aisle—displayed all the merchandise in the ad, plus more if we wish. We have highlighted a few items, showing them far more attractively, in color, than black and white drawings in the paper. We have created the impression of a big sale by displaying a mass of merchandise. We can, if we want, make several commercials, featuring different products in each one, giving us a two-day campaign with considerable excitement. And we have actually increased the readership and the value of Thrifty's newspaper advertising by some percentage, perhaps more than the TV salesman promised, although that generally takes some doing.

At this point you may be thinking: "Wouldn't it be impossible to show today's ad on TV today? What about production time?"

That's one of the delightful things about TV and radio: what you tape is ready to broadcast instantaneously. To accomplish what we have just roughed out, you would schedule a taping session for whenever the art for the newspaper ad was finished. Using the art or a photocopy, you would have your commercial taped and ready to broadcast a day or two before the paper went to press, if you wanted to. That's how easy it is.

There is one other technical device we probably would have used: chromakey, abbreviated CK or CHROMA or simply KEY. Chromakey is what you see behind Walter Cronkite with newsreel shots of the news as he describes the action. This rear screen effect is achieved electronically with a blue card, or blue drape cyclorama (abbreviated CYC) in front of which the announcer, or any other object, is positioned. Our use of this effect would probably have been to have superimposed, or SUPERED, the last scene over a photograph of an actual store interior, with SALE banners, etc., creating some excitement. Many viewers would assume that we had sent a TV camera crew out to the store, but in any case they would have accepted the illusion just as they accept the illusion of

Walter Cronkite sitting in front of the White House one minute, in front of the pyramids the next. (Abbreviation for superimpose is SUPER or SUP or sometimes MATTE, following motion picture terminology.) Chromakey backgrounds may be small, in which case they are called WINDOWS, or full screen (FS or FULL SCR), and the announcer can be made to appear as large or as small as we want. Most often, the scene that is to be used as a chromakey background is supplied to the station on a 35mm slide, but it can be on motion picture film, or it can be any object or person that you can aim a TV camera at while you are taping.

A technical point you should know about chromakey: Blue is usually the color used for the key (although another color can be used) because most studios have a blue drape (CYC, pronounced *sike).*

What happens is that any blue surface—WINDOW, CYC, anything that CAM #1 is looking at—is replaced by an image from CAM #2. This can have some funny effects. If an announcer is wearing a blue suit and a blue shirt and walks into a chromakey scene, his blue suit and shirt disappear and what appears on the screen is the announcer's head drifting around without a body. Generally, this is a nuisance. In an ECU of a blue-eyed announcer, we don't see any pupils in his eyes. In place of his pupils, we see the White House or Cairo or whatever is on chromakey. Surprisingly, this effect has never been used on purpose in commercials. Conceivably, you could have a commercial where a girl's eyes fade to a scene on a Caribbean island at the mention of the words "take a vacation cruise." Or any product that we want to show being thought of or desired. Far as I know, this has never been done. You can be the first if you like. It is my gift to you.

Using your new tools, plus the enumerate, manipulate, eliminate formula, go through the paper and look for ads you'd like to make into TV commercials. We've already tackled what I believe is the most difficult problem—converting a retail ad with many items to TV—so anything else you want to do should be easy. I suggest you try a supermarket, a department store and a specialty merchandise store, such as sporting goods, using only the devices we have just demonstrated in the Thrifty Drug commercial. This commercial would have been much improved without using all the effects that I included for demonstration purposes. So try a few with fewer effects.

WHAT ABOUT STORYBOARDS?

A storyboard, as you probably know, is a sort of comic strip visualizing a TV commercial. Storyboards are valueless in the actual production of TV commercials. Obviously, the director can't go running with a storyboard from one cameraman to another, from the sound technician to the technical director and the tape technician and the lighting people during the taping of a commercial. All his directions must be reduced to spoken words that can be transmitted over the communications system from the director's booth, using the abbreviated language that has been developed for that purpose.

But the storyboard does have one very important function: It is used to sell the commercial to the advertiser. Since that sale must take place before any money starts its happy journey to your pocket, you should get some practice in making storyboards. A sample is in this chapter. You might want to have one made up with your name at the top and take it to your neighborhood printer and have a few hundred run off, or you might Xerox a few.

If you can draw, or have a friend who can, you probably will not be able to resist making the storyboard a work of art in its own right. If you can't draw, as I cannot, you make stick figures. Actually, stick figures and sloppy drawings have some of the charm of kindergarten drawings, and tend to disarm whoever you're showing the storyboard to. Although I have access to artists, as you will have when you start writing commercials for stations or agencies, I use stick figure storyboards when it is necessary to submit commercials to government regulatory agencies precisely because they do not look slick. The theory is that anyone so innocent of artistic skill is probably without guile, probably is incapable of any artifice in the copy which would skirt FTC regulations.

But if you want to create storyboards suitable for hanging in the Metropolitan Museum of Art, enjoy yourself.

One small caution: if you do make a storyboard to go with your written commercial, don't show it to anyone in the business without a note or remark to this effect: "Here's a storyboard in case you need one for a presentation to a client." This lets them know you are not an amateur.

Most clients who do any TV advertising at all don't want to see storyboards, but you may be writing for advertisers who have never used TV before and feel lost without something resembling a newspaper layout that they can OK. Or they want a storyboard to show at a sales meeting.

So you can work either way—with or without storyboards—whichever makes you comfortable.

ACTING OUT THE COMMERCIAL

At some stage, you will probably find yourself reading your own copy aloud to someone. Unconsciously, you will find yourself making small body motions, gestures, and so on. You may think of yourself as painfully shy, but for reasons I do not understand, your self-consciousness will disappear on these occasions, and your voice will take on inflections that would do credit to Richard Burton or Ellen Burstyn.

Don't be surprised if whoever you're reading the copy to exclaims—like one of the characters in an old Deanna Durbin movie who would cry out: "Say! Why don't we put on our own show! Right here in this old barn!"—to you: "Why don't you do the commercial yourself? You really put the meaning across!"

WHY NOT?

There are lots of reasons why you should resist the temptation. No matter how much conviction you are able to put into the commercial, having written it and understanding it better than anyone else, don't underestimate the power of the professional announcer, actress or actor. They will put strengths, subtleties, poetry into their presentation of your copy that you did not suspect were there.

But it's also possible that the talent available at the station may be of the rip-and-read persuasion (the term comes from newcomers who do just that: rip and read, mindlessly, stories just as they come off the news printer). You may really and truly be the best person to do the commercial. If someone insists that you try it, do it.

There's one great argument for announcing your own commercials: money. Part of this chapter is a summary of AFTRA (American Federation of Television and Radio Artists) pay scales. Although the subject is complex—involving different scales for markets of different sizes, whether you are on camera or off camera, how many weeks the commercial is broadcast and so on—two things are generally true: you are well paid for 30 seconds' work, and you get paid again (the famous "residuals") every 13 weeks. And the pay scale speaks for itself.

RADIO AGAIN. We'll be jumping back and forth from radio to TV, because that's what you will be doing as a commercial writer.

Let's take this same problem—converting a newspaper ad with a lot of merchandise to a commercial—and see what we can do with radio.

Obviously, we can't show the ad. We can't build a set displaying all the merchandise. We don't have chromakey for a store background. Let's see what we do have.

Most important, we have our old friends, enumerate, manipulate, and eliminate, heavy on the eliminate.

And we have more time. Although TV commercials can be almost any length, they are usually 30 seconds. Radio commercials are usually 60 seconds. So that's a help.

We also have the fact that radio audiences tend to be fractionated. One radio station may be programmed for teenagers, with hard rock. Another, a talk or news station, is aimed more at adults, or older adults. There are sports program formats aimed at men, service formats aimed at women, and so on. There are so many radio stations that there is an opportunity to tailor commercials to a particular audience, selecting only the products—from all those listed in the newspaper ad—that have strong appeal for the station broadcasting the advertising.

LEARN FROM JUNGLE SAM

There is a trap here. Sooner or later, someone is certain to say to you: "It isn't enough to pick the merchandise or the particular offer that appeals to a particular group. What we need is special copy for each station, using the special language of each group; you see, each group thinks differently, and what you write for one audience will have just the opposite meaning for another group, etc."

One of the legends of Hollywood is Sam Katzman, better known as Jungle Sam. Jungle Sam produced dozens, perhaps hundreds, of movies. Almost alone among producers, he never made a move that didn't make money. For years, he made jungle movies along the lines of Tarzan. When the public developed an interest in space, Sam called Central Costume and said, "I'm returning the ape suits and safari outfits; send me some space suits, same size." And periodically he did the same thing for gangster suits, western costumes, whatever was selling.

He'd scratch out "leopard" or "tiger" here and there in the script and substitute "asteroid" or "android" or "outlaw" according to what kind of picture he was making that week, but otherwise he never changed a thing, certainly not the plot, which was the basic "rape, ride and revenge" formula. Never made a picture that didn't make money.

But frequently a producer or actor or director or writer who had gone bankrupt on a movie would come to Jungle Sam for a job. "Sam," they would generally begin, "what you don't understand"—(isn't it remarkable how dumb people spend most of their lives telling intelligent people they don't understand?)—"Sam, what you don't understand is that you can't make a space picture the way you do, with the same plot you use for a western or a jungle movie. The people who come to a space epic don't respond to the same things."

"Son," Jungle Sam would say gently, "they all got the same glands," and continue on his way to the bank.

Common sense tells us Jungle Sam is right. People are more alike than they are different. They all get hungry, thirsty, tired, lustful, angry, restless, for about the same reasons. They rejoice at their own occasional good fortune, lament the injustice of not getting a raise, getting a traffic ticket, paying taxes. They wish they looked like Robert Redford or Katherine Deneuve. If you introduce a commercial with the screech of brakes or a shrill police whistle, you get their attention, whether they are old or young, rich or poor, Hindu, Jew or Christian. So avoid this trap if you can.

But sometimes you cannot. Sometimes that's your assignment—write special commercials for teenagers, blue collar workers, classical music listeners, etc. And you have to do it, or move on to another job.

If you can write in the patois of each group without a false note, do it. If you're a good writer, you might also try your hand at a Broadway play (but don't invest in it; back Sam Katzman instead.)

Fortunately, there's a simple solution: the Fact Sheet. You simply enumerate the elements you would normally put in a commercial, (having first eliminated some and manipulated the ones you selected into an order that makes sense, and type it up in outline form with instructions for the ANNCR to *ad lib around this FACT SHEET in your own style.* The station announcer will use whatever language he normally uses on his show, addressing whatever kind of audience he thinks he has. And you are spared the trouble of writing a commercial; you just type up your outline of a commercial, write FACT SHEET at the top, and relax.

FX AND SFX

You can avoid a lot of silly discussions about changing mores, peer groups, intellectual versus emotional appeal (remind me of this later) and other prattle about the number of angels on the head of a pin by doing one simple thing: *make your commercials jump out of the tube, out of the speaker* so there's no argument about their compelling attention.

One easy way to do this is with FX (effects) or SFX (sound effects).

Included in this chapter is a list of SFX and where to get them.

Now, for the first time since you started on this project with me, we're going to have some fun. Let's go back to our old friend the car dealer and see what we can do with some SFX.

Consider that pedestrian statement in the copy we fooled around with before: "You'll never know you get the best deal unless...."

Close your eyes and stick a pin in the list of SFX. I'll do the same. I happened to hit LAUGHTER. Let's try it.

SFX: Laughter, establish 3 secs and under ANNCR:
Do you want people laughing at you? Making fun of you because you paid hundreds of dollars more than you should for a new car?
UP SFX & UNDER
You'll never know whether you got the best deal, or paid hundreds of dollars more than you should have unless you...

What did you hit? CREAKING DOOR? Try it.
SFX: Creaking door, establish & under ANNCR (echo chamber, filter for eerie FX)

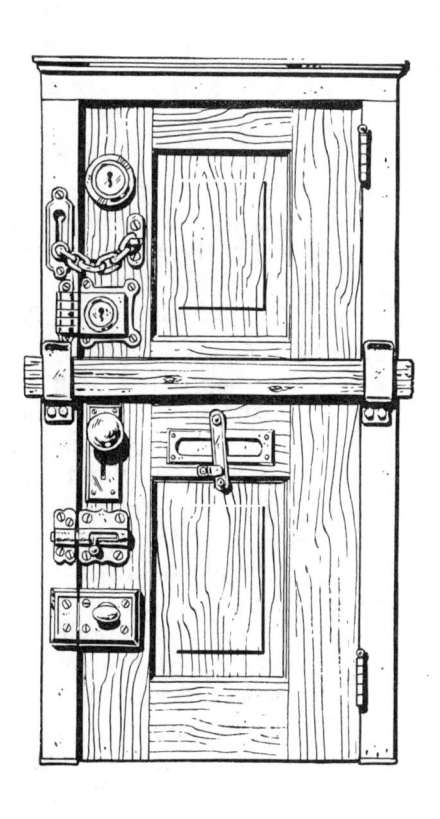

You'll never know, will you. Never...really...know... never know if you've been a victim...never know if you've paid too much...hundreds of dollars too much...for a new car unless...unless you take off right now....

SOUND OF CAR DIGGING OUT, ACCELERATING, SEGUE TO SCREECHING TIRES AROUND CORNER, MORE ACCELERATION...

and so on. You can combine any number of SFX, letting one fade under while another fades in (this is called a SEGUE).

Included in this chapter is an example (Perkin-Elmer, recruiting) of how a rifle shot and ricochet SFX was used to get attention and make the point that the appeal is selective. This commercial delivered qualified applicants in several markets for a fraction of the cost of a big space newspaper classified campaign.

The Boeing recruiting commercial used the seagull SFX to attract attention and to underscore the unique environment that Boeing offers engineers.

I won't waste space and your time here with more examples. Make your own. Pick any advertiser and run down the list of SFX and see what they suggest. Just think about commercials using SFX for the moment, outlining a few if you feel like it, for the fun of it.

There's another FX you should be thinking about now, too, either to use by itself or in conjunction with SFX. Music. MUSIC FX. Part of this chapter is a sample catalog sheet of cleared music that you can use in commercials. Without going into the rules regarding performers' and composers' rights and royalties, you can find about any kind of music *cleared for broadcast* (hence the term "cleared music") on which all fees have been paid. There is a charge, commonly priced "per needle drop" although of course most of the cleared libraries are on tape, which the station or producer pays and then adds to the production bill for the spot. Some of the music is so impressive, with so many instruments, that producers and writers who produce their own commercials have been known to charge hundreds, even thousands, of dollars for it rather than the typical $50 needle drop fee. Let your conscience battle your avarice on this.

Now it's time to write a commercial, using both SFX and MUSIC FX. Among the many classifications that lend themselves to this are resorts, travel, restaurants.

Typical openings are:

SFX: Crash, breaking glass, screams, traffic, honking, sirens, cut dead.

ANNCR: Stop. Think a minute about the noise, the congestion, the stress you endure every day. What's it doing to you?

SFX: Sneak in same SFX under ANNCR
Isn't it time you said: Stop!
SFX: All SFX stop, dead
and treated yourself to a
(MUSIC FX CAP HI-Q REEL M-88 CUT –PASTORAL, VIOLINS, UP & UNDER ANNCR)

...weekend somewhere, a cruise, an evening at a restaurant, whatever advertiser you're working on. Try a commercial now, using SFX and MUSIC FX. Probably you will want to end the commercial with a quick repetition of your SFX, or bring the music up alone, whatever works best.

Now, you don't have to concern yourself with buying any of these SFX or MUSIC FX. All you have to do is write them into the copy. In this example, to show you the style, I wrote CAP HI-Q REEL M-88 #4, which happens to be a pastoral theme.

You might take the same resort, airline, cruise line or restaurant and use an entirely different SFX, MUSIC FX combination to build a commercial with a different appeal. Instead of appealing to the person who's enduring a lot of urban pressure, let's appeal to lonely people, of whom there are many.

Here's an example of how SFX and MUSIC SFX can do something we wouldn't dare do in copy. We couldn't very well start out with a straightforward appeal to wallflowers, like this:

Friends, are you lonely? unpopular? are you sitting in your apartment right now, wondering if the phone will ever ring? Listen. There's a place you can go to meet people, maybe even someone who would like to marry you....

Mind you, this copy would work very well. But the resort or airline or cruise line or restaurant wouldn't let you broadcast it because they don't want to create the feeling that only the lost, lonely, friendless misfits and outcasts are their customers, even though that may be the truth. But they do know that loneliness and the hope of finding love are often what motivate people to take cruises, go out to dinner and so on. Let's use MUSIC and SFX to do what we can't put in words:

MUSIC FX: Tinkling piano, cocktail music, hold under SFX clinking glasses, murmur of conversation, muted feminine laughter, establish and under ANNCR: (Laughing slightly, as if turning away from a conversation)—*you know what I like best about (name of restaurant, cruise ship, resort, whatever). Waiting to be served. I've met more great people here, standing around the fireplace, waiting for a table. Just small talk, you know, but it's such a friendly place, people kind of introduce themselves. Why, I remember one time. . . .*

Obviously, by picking the music—cocktail piano, singing piano bar, disco—you can select the age group, the type of people: solid citizens, swingers, young couples, businessmen on the town, singles, whatever you want to attract. Impossible to do this subtly in newspapers. That makes it easy for a station to sell this campaign on radio or TV, easy for you to make money writing new commercials in the series.

Back to TV. Take this same situation—use the same FX, or pick out others, as you wish—and convert it to a 30-second TV commercial. Write the opening only.

You probably have something like this:

1 Man turns away from small group, turns to camera as if camera is another person chromakeyed over scene other people in similar BG groups in iris down for low key light in BG scene	MUSIC FX: Tinkling piano, SFX ice in glasses *(Copy same as in radio version)*

And that's all there is to it. Now, why did I specify Chromakey as the background? Why not simply have other groups of people milling about? Budget. Refer to your AFTRA scale in this chapter and see how much it would cost to add the twenty or thirty people it would take to make the scene effective. Since they're in the background, anyway, a still photo from the advertiser's file, with the light level low, will do the trick. If the viewer notices that the other people aren't moving—which would be a distraction we don't want—it will be assumed that the effect is deliberate.

EYE CONTACT

In this quick TV knockoff of the radio copy, we have used what is probably the most powerful single device in TV: eye contact. The announcer turns and looks at the camera as if it were a person.

I said at the beginning that this was not a textbook on broadcasting, and we would deal with practice, not theory. But we should take a moment to talk about the eye contact theory of TV.

In TV dramatic programs, the writers and director operate on the proscenium theory, as if in a stage play or a movie. The proscenium theory is that one wall of the room where the action is taking place has been removed, and we are eavesdropping on the actors, who are unaware of our presence. This is a terrible simplification of a couple of thousand years of tradition of drama, but it's enough for our purpose.

If you think of TV commercials as miniature movies or Broadway plays, that's what you do: pretend that a wall has been removed and we are watching those boring, unbelievable little playlets without the actresses being aware of our presence. A friend of mine who has been in lots of them says he never has to learn any lines because he never does anything but open the door and say, "Hi, Hon! I'm home! What's for dinner?" followed by his mute reactions to her rhapsodizing about some new margarine.

Now, people will put up with this in a theater (and many plays, face it, are worse than commercials of equal length) because they have paid to get in and can't get out without stepping on somebody's feet.

But the TV audience is free to get up and go to the refrigerator. Since the actors are unaware of their presence, their feelings can't possibly be hurt, so it's OK to walk out on them. It's that simple.

When someone looks you in the eye, however, looks directly at you and speaks directly to you, it's hard to look away. If the announcer is any good, you would feel yourself guilty of rudeness if you walked out on him. You might also feel it a sign of weakness if you were unable to look him in the eye.

I know, you do it all the time, and so do I. But it's a little harder than walking out on a faceless announcer narrating a scene for us, or a couple of ladies discussing detergents with each other. That may be why you see fewer VO-Voice Over—commercials than you used to.

VO commercials are easier to make in some ways, and easier to edit, which covers up a lot of sloppiness in the writing and producing. They're more profitable to produce for these reasons, and many people in the business understandably prefer to produce VO's.

ORDER NOW, OR ELSE!

One type of advertiser who practically never uses VO's is the direct response advertiser. Typically, he wants you to phone at the end of the commercial "for more information" or for a brochure. The last thing you see in these commercials is the phone number, full screen. Now, that phone number is unlisted, a number used only on TV, only at that time. If the advertiser gets 53 calls on that line, he knows those calls came from that commercial, and nowhere else. If he paid $100 for the time, he divides 53 into $100 and discovers that it cost him $1.89 to get each phone call. If you write a commercial for him that produces 236 phone calls, he divides 236 into $100 and discovers each call cost him only 42 cents, and you are the new writer. But if you write a commercial that delivers only 9 phone calls—and the differences in results can be that great—he notes that his cost per call is $11.11, and a man appears at your office door to scrape your name off it.

So writers of direct response commercials tend to do only what produces the most results, and their commercials are generally eye contact. In this chapter are a couple of examples. Note that there is only one video direction involving the announcer: MCU (Medium closeup). The idea is to put someone in your living room at a conversational distance and keep him there as if he were facing you across your coffee table.

You may or may not want to write this terribly exacting kind of commercial, but the money is good because successful commercials usually run a long time. I mention this kind of commercial because it usually has three elements you should know about.

BALLY, TIP AND TURN

Besides enumerate, eliminate and manipulate, which are a way of organizing material, there is the structure of the commercial, the classic bally, tip, turn.

These terms come from the carnival midway, which has much in common with the parade of peddlers through your living room. BALLY is to call attention to your pitch, one meaning of which is your tent, or booth. The TIP is the crowd. The carny talker (barker in a carnival) BALLIES UP A TIP, does something to get a crowd (TIP) to his PITCH. He may bring out a sword swallower or fire eater or some dancing girls; he may fire off a blank pistol or set fire to a newspaper and wave it in the air. He may simply single you out with eye contact, walk along with you, talking directly to you, persuading you to stop, then repeat the process until he has collected the nucleus of a TIP, when he starts his demonstration of the glass cutter or the cabbage slicer. But when the free show—the dancing girls, the demonstration, is over—he must TURN THE TIP.

He must get the TIP, the crowd, marching to the ticket window and into the tent, or reaching in their pockets for cash to buy the cabbage slicer.

Obviously, turning the tip is the object of the game. At some point in every commercial that means business, the tip is turned. In the direct response commercials in this chapter, it's easy to see where the tip is turned. Even easier, because I have inserted a / in each commercial to show where the tip is turned. Not only in those, but in the other sample commercials in this chapter. Take a look.

This evening, make it a point to watch for the turning of the tip; listen for it in radio. In the hands of a master, it is hard to know when the change takes place, but it is there.

Often it is the shift to the word YOU. The commercial rambles along, explaining how fine the product or service is, and then the tone changes to "how about you?" wouldn't you like to have (whatever it is) in your home (garage, safe deposit box, whatever)? Here's what you do....

All commercials do not have all three elements. It can be argued that Merv Griffin or Barbara Walters has already ballied up the tip, drawn the crowd to your pitch. In that case, all you have to do is turn the tip. Many commercials do this: start turning the tip from the top.

But turning the tip—urging some kind of action—is the one ingredient you can't eliminate, unless the advertiser doesn't care what happened to his money.

Now take a look at ads in the paper, or in TV Guide, or any publication that carries a lot of coupon advertising, and see what you can do with a direct response commercial on radio or TV. Use eye contact, or its equivalent in radio— an opening like, "Hey, listen to this!"—simple, direct, amazingly effective. Use FX only if you must. Come in early for a closeup of the booklet or whatever is being offered (or start talking about it in the radio commercial), stay with it to the end and hit the phone number twice if on TV, thrice if on radio. Then stop. Add nothing. No slogan, or final injunction to "do it now" and never, never add a log or sig, visual, musical or otherwise.

When you've hit the phone number the last time, quit. Quit while you're ahead.

Now take this commercial—no matter how inelegant you think it is—following this formula exactly, and mail it to the sales manager of a station in your area. Clip to it the ad you've adapted, and this note from you (phone the station first and learn how to spell the sales manager's name).

Dear XXXXXXX,

I think (Call letters of the station) can deliver qualified responses cheaper for this advertiser, using a commercial like this one. (Name of advertiser) spent $00000* to run this in the (Name of publication). If you'd like to have this money spent on your station instead, please call me.

*Obviously you call the publication and find out what an ad that size costs to run.

If you want to write commercials like this for money, write a commercial like this today. Mail it tomorrow. If you don't have an answer in a week, which I think you will, send the same thing to another station and repeat until you get a call, and an offer to do some writing for the station.

Now go back to the first pages in this chapter. Pick another classification. Write a commercial for it, using what you have learned, referring to the Dictionary of Terms, using FX, SFX, MUSIC FX where you think you should. Write them in as if you had them. Don't worry, the station will find them for you.

Follow the same procedure: clip out the ad, attach it to your commercial, and send the same letter to the same sales managers (changing only the phrase "qualified responses" to "customers", "car buyers," "beer drinkers," or whatever it is they're looking for.

Don't worry. You'll get answers, interviews if you want them, and writing assignments.

FREE PRODUCTION, TALENT, MUSIC

The actual cost of taping a commercial at a radio station or TV station is approximately $0. In fact, many stations produce commercials: announcer, music, special effects, free as an inducement to get or keep an advertiser. This is true mainly of stations that are having trouble selling time, of course, but there are plenty of them, and they are the people you should be talking to about getting your commercials produced free.

Here's a procedure to follow. Pick a substantial newspaper advertiser who is not on radio or TV. Study what the advertiser is doing, particularly what customers he is trying to reach: old, young, men, women, rich, poor, whatever. Let's take a personal small loan company as an example.

Most of the readers of the newspaper are wasted circulation for this advertiser, assuming they even read his ad. In fact, clip his ad from the paper on a day when it is buried in the gutter between two big ads, or next to a competitor, or on a day when the newspaper reproduced it poorly, or all of the above.

Call the loan company and find out who's in charge. Be sure it's the top man or woman, the president or general manager. Don't say why you want the information. Say you want to write him a letter. Get the spelling by all means. Let's say it's Smythe.

Write a commercial using the facts from this ad, but using some dramatic sound effects, or music, or both. Use two, three announcers, whatever you need to develop your idea. Don't worry about the expense, because you're not going to spend a nickel. Make a rough storyboard if you like.

Then pick out a station with programming which common sense tells you reaches the kind of folks a loan company would want to talk to. Call the manager of the station and tell him you have an irresistible idea which will make this company an advertiser on that station. But "before presenting it to Mr. Smythe" you would like to show it to the station sales manager and get his cooperation. Don't give him the idea over the phone, or discuss it. Insist on an appointment. Don't worry, you'll get it (or go to his competitor).

When you discuss it with the sales manager, ask him if he has talent on the station who could produce an audition tape for Mr. Smythe. He will assume that you have some acquaintance with Mr. Smythe, but it's OK if he realizes you have not. The mere fact that you have the name suggests that you do things in a businesslike way.

Tell him how much you want for the commercial—say $500—but you don't expect a nickel unless Smythe's company becomes an advertiser, spending enough to justify your fee. Tell him you're speculating your time, that you'd like to build a relationship with the station where you help them get new advertisers in just this way. All he has to do is speculate the production, using people who are standing around anyway, and music and effects that are gathering dust in the station. Obviously, you want him or a station salesman to make the presentation to Mr. Smythe on the station's coverage, pointing out—aided by the newspaper clipping you have—the terrible treatment he's getting from the paper.

The station manager would be a fool not to accept your offer, regardless of your lack of experience. It isn't every day that someone comes in to him with an idea, backed by some work already done, that will get his station more business. Don't be surprised if he offers to put you on a retainer, or make some other arrangement that will keep you interested in helping the station do more business.

And they'll tape your commercial. Whether Mr. Smythe ever goes on the station or not, you'll have a sample of your own work, professionally produced. A good thing to have.

If you're in a position to travel or possibly relocate, repeat the process (find a magazine or newspaper ad, or take notes from a commercial on the air) on national products. The process, the terminology, the tricks of the trade are identical, except it's easier than writing retail, automotive, direct response and other local advertising. In this case, write the national headquarters of the advertiser and ask to be referred to their agency. They will do it; don't worry. No company ever got mad at anyone who volunteers to try to help sell their product. The agency may not be able to use the particular commercial you have written, but they may have other clients they need writing for, right now.

Don't be shy about phoning anyone you have written to. "Did you get the commercial I sent you? What did you think?" Listen to their comments, rewrite your commercial accordingly and send it back to them. That's what all of us who write commercials do, all the time: write and rewrite.

If you've followed the step-by-step plans all the way to this point; if you've done the assignments, don't waste any time trying to absorb more theory. I could write another thousand pages about theories, techniques, case histories. But knowing what I know won't put a nickel in your pocket. Get busy writing. No matter how amateurish you think it is, there's something worse on the air right now, and someone got paid for doing it.

The rest of this chapter has the technical terms, sample commercials, lists of stations, producers, agencies, even the basic forms you need to reproduce to set up shop.

Go to work. You're as ready as you'll ever be until you get some of your work out in the marketplace and begin to hear it, see it on the air.

Don't be discouraged after a few refusals. I had plenty, we all had plenty. Stick with it and you'll be sitting in a study like mine, overlooking the Blue Ridge Mountains and a fantastic swimming pool, living the good life, the easy life.

When you've cashed your first checks, if you think of it, drop me a note and tell me about it. Good luck. Get busy.

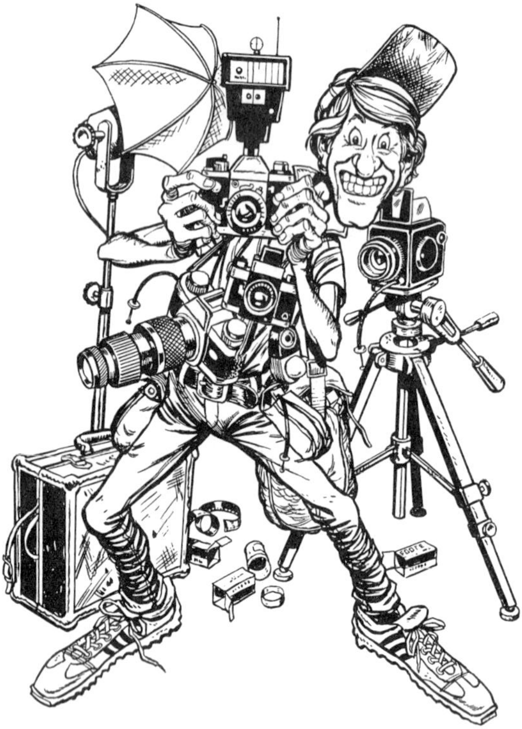

DICTIONARY OF BROADCAST TERMS

DICTIONARY OF TERMS

AAAA: American Association of Advertising Agencies
A-B ROLLING: for editing, film or tape is put on two reels, alternating the scenes to be used
ACADEMY LEADER: film with markings one second apart which is spliced at beginning of reel
ACCOUNT: customer. An advertiser is the account of an advertising agency, the agency is the station's account.
ACETATE: celluloid-like sheet, usually called "cell" used in animated cartoon, other art production
A.D.: Assistant Director
AE: shortest distance between two ulcers; also known as Account Executive
AFFILIATE: a station now owned by a network that contracts to carry network programs
AFTRA: American Federation of Television and Radio Artists (union)
AGVA: American Guild Variety Artists (union)
AGMA: American Guild Musical Artists (union)
ANN or ANNCR: Announcer
ANGLE SHOT: shot made from different angle than preceding scene, or from any unusual angle
APERTURE: lens opening, F-stop
AUTHOR'S TITLE: usually follows Director's Title in program credits
ARC: to dolly in or out on a curving path
ASCAP: American Society of Composers, Authors and Publishers. Collects royalties for them. Music primarily, but could be other copyrighted material.
ASPECT RATIO: shape of TV image: 3 deep, 4 wide
AUDIO: sound
A-WIND: tape or film wound with emulsion inside
BACK LIGHT: just what it sounds like: lighting from behind the subject. Big in shampoo commercials.
BACKGROUND LIGHT: different from Back Light. Background Light is lighting set or objects in the background, furniture, etc.
BACK PROJECTION or REAR SCREEN PROJECTION: image projected on translucent screen as background. Nearly obsolete; replaced by Chroma Key.
BACK TIMING: counting the time left instead of the time elapsed during a commercial or show

BALOP: a card or roll, usually titles, on which a camera chain is permanently focused
BARN DOORS: metal flaps around lights
BEANER: Spanish language station
BG: background. Used mostly in radio or audio for TV, as in "FADE MUSIC TO BG." Also in video, as in "CLOTHING RACKS, SHELVES IN BG"
BIK: a commercial where two ladies entertain each other discussing detergents, margarine, floor wax, whatever. BIK stands for Broads in Kitchen
BLACK: black. "Go to black" is a way of ending a scene to prepare for supering a number or sig
BLOCKING: talking through, sometimes walking through main movements of people and equipment
BMI: like ASCAP, same function
BOOK: hinged background flat that opens like a book
BOOM: long pole from which microphone or camera and operator hang
BROAD: a square floodlight
BRIDGING TITLE: title in middle of a commercial, as in 20 MINUTES LATER to show how white wash gets
BURN or BURN-IN: after image if camera is left focused on same object too long
BUS: buttons on video control panel, an audio circuit
CAMERA: sometimes called Box, as in "how many boxes we got on this commercial?"
CAMERA CHAIN: the box plus power supply and anything it may be permanently focused on, such as a movie or slide projector
CAMERA LIGHT: small light mounted on camera, sometimes called "inky-dinky." For illumination of scene; not the red light which tells performers which camera is taking the scene at the moment
CAMERA REHEARSAL: dress rehearsal with cameras on but not broadcasting
CAMERA LEFT, RIGHT: direction to cameraman. In TV, it is from the cameraman's point of view, not the action, as in stage directions
CAPTURE: in videotape recording, this is what the operator says to the director when the image and sound appear properly on the small monitor camera of the machine receiving the signal: "we have a capture" means OK

CATV: Cable TV. Terms comes from Community Antenna TV, which preceded cable
CCTV: Closed Circuit TV
CHEAT; turn slightly toward the camera; instead of facing each other in a dialogue, performers "cheat" toward the camera
CHROMA KEY: this has replaced the old rear screen projection. A background scene appears electronically behind the performer or object. Generally, this is done with a blue screen, but other colors may be used.
CHROMINANCE: red, green and blue circuits; everything but black in color TV
CLIENT: the advertiser
CLIP: film or tape that has been physically cut to a short length for editing
CLOSEUP: CU is abbreviation you use
COAX: coaxial cable, shielded wire
COLD LIGHT: flourescent
COMPOSITE: more than one image broadcast at the same time, split screen; also the complete TV signal including sound and sync pulse, an electronic signal that keeps it all together
CONTROL ROOM: where the TD—technical director—sits, where the equipment is that puts it all together
CRANE SHOT: same as BOOM shot in TV, but more common in film production. Camera and operator are lifted above scene
CRAWL: names, numbers, anything printed that is made to crawl across a title card, but sometimes by focusing on a drum over which the printed material is rolled. Technically, crawl used to mean only side-to-side movement and up-and-down movement was called "roll" but this distinction is no longer observed
CREDITS: names of everybody who participated in a show. As a commercial writer, do not expect this immortality.
CROSSCUT: cut from one scene to another, back and forth, to show simultaneous action. Dangerous unless you are deliberately trying for laughs because it suggests and was once known as the "Griffith last-minute rescue."
CUCALORUS: "cookie" or "scrim"—a pattern achieved by projecting a light through a cutout screen onto a background

CUE: word or motion that tells announcer or camera or audio or lighting or musician or editor or anybody else to start doing something, or stop
CUT: instant switch from one scene to another
CYC: cyclorama, a backdrop, generally curved, usually blue
CUT-IN: a still picture edited in—usually as the commercial is being taped—sometimes of the product, but more generally of a sign or emblem accompanying a line like "wherever you see the familiar orange-and-purple seagull"
DEAD: not in operation, as "dead camera"—usually equipment, but on occasion as a direction in your copy, as in "ANNCR STOPS DEAD AS SHE DETECTS SCENT OF ROOM DEODORIZER"
DEFINITION: sharpness of image
DEPTH, DEPTH OF FIELD: according to lens and F-stop, cameras can focus only on subjects within a certain range. Often you specify this to concentrate the viewer's attention on what is in focus. Make this a separate direction, not in body of commercial copy.
DEPTH STAGING: separating scene into foreground, middle ground and background
DIMMER: rheostat that controls brightness of lighting
DIM BULB: a radio or TV station of low power
DISH: reflector for transmitting unit
DISSOLVE: go from one picture to another by overlapping images. Can be fast or slow dissolve. Can be accomplished by going out of focus on one picture while going into focus on the next, or simply by overlapping without losing focus
DISTORTION: just what it sounds like. Can be used deliberately as special effect video or audio by using, for example, a telephoto lens, which makes things in the near distance actually look larger than things that are in fact the same size and closer. There is a big range of audio distortions, from echo to filters that simulate phones, etc.
DISTANCE SHOT: mainly a film term, not used much in TV. In TV, it is WS, or Wide Shot
DOLLY: the word comes from a wheeled cart. In film, you call for the camera to DOLLY IN or DOLLY OUT. In TV, it's PUSH IN, PULL OUT. Big deal. Sometimes called FOLLOW SHOT, TRACKING SHOT, TRUCKING SHOT. Purists limit DOLLY to in or out; sideways motions are PANS.

DOUBLE SYSTEM: film term for putting sound and picture on separate films and combining later
DOUBLE EXPOSURE: one picture on top of another
DOWNSTAGE: towards the camera
DREAM BALLOON: showing the character's thoughts in an area above his head
DRESS: to get something in the set ready to tape, as in "Dress that painting on the wall; it's hanging crooked"
DROP: backdrop
DRY RUN: rehearse without cameras
DUB: copy. Duplicate tapes, called DUBS or DUPES, are made from original, or MASTER
DUTCHMAN: hinges, usually canvas, painted same as scenery (FLAT) so it can be folded
DYNAMIC: Common type of microphone
ECU: extreme closeup. Also XCU
EDITING: two kinds. One, the tape or film is cut; the other, scenes are taken away or added electronically: ELECTRONIC EDIT
ESTABLISHING SHOT: Wide Shot (WS) establishing where we are before going to closeups

ELEVATION: drawing of a set from ground level, not schematic as if seen from above
ESSENTIAL AREA: the portion of the picture that actually will appear on the home screen; it cuts off a little around the edges of what you see on the monitor in the studio
ET: old term for the type of record (Electrical Transcription) once used on radio. Tape has replaced the ET except for some SFX (Sound Effects) libraries, and some music
ETV: Educational Television. Also obsolete. These stations are now called Public Television. They do use commercials, mainly for their own programming hypes (in commercial TV, hypes are sometimes called STAY-TUNEDS) and for their fund-raising events, and for some products "contributed" along with money for TV exposure. Don't eliminate Public TV from your list of customers; they often have rate cards, just like commercial stations, because they do sell time, although the word commercial is distasteful to them. Somebody has to be paid for writing those GRANT IDs (equivalent to COMMERCIAL IDs—Identification

spots—on commercial TV) identifying the company that pays the bill. Most Public Television spots are written by their salaried staff, so freelancers have a hard time. But staff jobs do open up, and they're worth going after because they pay more than commercial stations, since they get tax money.

FACT SHEET: outline from which ANNCR ad libs

FAST MOTION: actions speeded up photographically or electronically

FADE-IN, FADE-OUT: gradually disclosing a scene or ending it by varying the light. Same for audio, radio, bringing volume up or down. Typical: ESTABLISH MUSIC, THEN FADE ON AUDIO CUE AND HOLD IN BG TO CC (hold in background to conclusion)

FLASH BACK: scene interrupting action with recall of earlier event. Rare in TV commercials of 30-sec length, but a useful device, as in, say, a hand lotion commercial where the lady muses about how her husband used to rave about how soft her hands were (FLASH BACK TO SCENE #4) but now all he does is go bowling

FX: effect, effects, special effect, radio or TV

FEEDBACK: in audio, the howling sound you hear when a microphone picks up the sound from a speaker; in TV, the picture streaks and flashes

FIELD: half the complete scanning cycle. Thus there are 60 fields per second, 30 frames per second.

FRAME: single photographic or electronic impression. In film, there are 16 frames—like tiny snapshots—per foot (35mm film). At 90 feet per minute, this is 24 frames per second. In TV, there are 30 frames per second.

FLARE: unwanted light flashes, which show up dark, caused by light reflecting off shiny or white objects; correct with dulling spray, by angling object so it does not reflect, or lighting

FLASH: extremely short shot, perhaps second or less

FLAT: standing scenery, as distinct from DROP or CYC

FLIP CARD: title card, to be flipped, or pulled, in sequence as camera stays in fixed focus. In connection with this is another meaning of FIELD. This FIELD is the amountof blank card surrounding whatever is printed on the card. If you don't have enough FIELD, the thumb of whoever is flipping the cards will be in the picture

FLOODLIGHT: a spotlight that lights a wider area
FLOOR: the studio floor, as distinct from the booth
FLOOR MEN: production crew
FLY: scenery or object hung (FLOWN) from above FLOOR
FORTY-MILER: an agency, advertiser, individual or proposition of some impermanence. A circus term from the days when a show could move 40 miles in a day, and very often had to, sheriff in pursuit.
GRP: Gross Rating Points, or total audience
GAIN: level, or volume, of sound. "Riding gain" is what the audio man does: turn the volume up or down. "Too much gain" just means too loud
GEN LOCK: synchronizing generators; if you don't, the picture rolls
GHOST: double image, usually referring to poor reception, where the same image is reflected back into the set, unlike DOUBLE EXPOSURE
GOBO: a foreground piece, such as a lattice or a plant that the camera shoots through: foreground
GO TO BLACK: fade out picture
GROUP SHOT: group of people in scene
GRIP: (also SCHLEPPER) laborer on set or floor
HALO: FLARE all around an object
HAND PROP: small prop handled by ANNCR
HEAD ROOM: space between top of ANNCR's head and top of screen
HIGH BAND COLOR: superior kind of electronic dub
HIGH KEY: strong lighting
HOLY FACTOR: supplemental light to fill in holes
HOT: turned on
HOT SPOT: too much light in one spot
IATSE: International Alliance of Theatrical Stage Employees (union)
IBEW: International Brotherhood of Electrical Workers (union)
ICONOSCOPE: obsolete. Old type TV camera tube
ID: Identification. Station ID, Spot ID, etc.
IDIOT SHEET: prompter with lines for ANNCR to read. Used to be cards held by floor man next to camera. Replaced by IDIOT SHEET on a roll, like a paper towel roll. Now mostly replaced by an electronic device called TELEPROMPTER or TELECUE, which projects the copy

on a slanted piece of glass over the camera lens so that ANNCR can look directly into camera as he reads

INTERCOM: communication system between director and crew, between floor and booth

INTERSYNC: electronic control bringing different video sources together

INSERT: cut-in. A scene, generally a product closeup, taped first, then edited in as if in ANNCR's hand. Lets ANNCR concentrate on PITCH without worrying about stopping to hold the package steady

IN THE CAN: finished tape or film. Term is not used very much; replaced by "that's a KEEPER" meaning we will keep that take, or "that's our MASTER" meaning that's the version we will keep and make our dubs from. IN THE CAN is now used mostly in answer to the question: "where the hell did the audio man go?"

IRIS: lens opening that can be made larger or smaller. Also FX where an image starts as a pinpoint and grows to fill the screen (IRIS IN) or the reverse (IRIS OUT)

KEY: in lighting, the intensity, or name of the principal light source. Also short for CHROMA KEY. Also, superimpose, as in KEY PHONE NUMBER OVER PACKAGE

KICKER LIGHT: supplemental lighting from side or back

KINE, KINESCOPE: obsolete. Film made off TV receiver

LAPEL: tiny microphone that clips to lapel

LAVALIERE: tiny microphone worn around neck

LEVEL: volume of sound or picture

LIMBO: object photographed or taped against black or neutral background, generally for INSERT

LAP DISSOLVE: older term, from film, for DISSOLVE from one scene to another by overlapping. Still in use.

LIP SYNC: synchronization of lip movement and speech. Film term. In TV, LIP SYNC is automatic.

LOG: record kept of everything broadcast, every day

LS: long shot. More common is WS, Wide Shot

LOW KEY: low lighting

MAG TRACK: sound stripe on film, alongside picture

MARK: chalk or masking tape marking where ANNCR should stand

MC: medium closeup. If you knew only one TV term, this would get you through most commercial writing. It is chest

and face, the most conversational distance for an ANNCR to be from the viewer and generall the best
MIXER: Audio control, TV or radio
MONITOR: TV receivers in studio. MASTER MONITOR show picture actually being taped
MS: medium shot, medium distance
MONTAGE: series of scenes linked by some special FX, such as turning of pages of book; also more than one picture on the screen at once, say 4 or 6 or 8, perhaps popping on and off. Fairly easy to do, and impressive to amateurs because it looks like a costly effect. But it doesn't work very well because it is distracting; you can't follow six actions at once any more than you can pay attention to six people taking at once.

MULTIPLEX: a way of broadcasting FM in stereo. No one has ever produced stereo commercials. You could be first.
MULTIPLEXER: bunch of mirrors, one way of achieving a montage
NAB: National Association of Broadcasters. The NAB Code spells out some do's and don'ts, most of which common sense tells you anyway, plus your own observation of what is being and not being broadcast. Lotteries, for example, are illegal (except where a State has gone into the business), so you can't advertise them. A few businesses, such as astrology, are legal and do advertise in newspapers, but can't on stations that subscribe to the Code. Best to check with the station you're getting involved with; they may be non-Code anyway, or the Code may have changed while you are reading this.
NABET: National Association of Broadcast Employees and Technicians (union)
NTSC: a set of technical standards to ensure uniformity in picture quality, cynically believed to stand for Never Twice Same Color
NET: network
OFF CAMERA: term used mostly in program production, not commercials, where VO, Voice Over, is used to describe a scene where the ANNCR is heard but not seen, where he narrates
OSCILLOSCOPE or SCOPE: small screen that shows electronic patterns representing technical elements of transmis-

sion. In TV, a SCOPE shows the RASTER, covered later
PA: Public Address loudspeaker system
PAN: side-to-side movement of camera
PATCHING: connecting varius circuits into one
PERSPECTIVE: in audio, making sure things that look far away sound far away
PICKUP: origin or picture or sound
PITCH: the principal sales argument of a commercial, as in "a two-for-one sale pitch"
POT: potentiometer. The knob they turn to regulate audio volume
PREVIEW: looking at a scene on a PREVIEW MONITOR before it is taped or telecast, sometimes only a second before it is switched to tape or transmitter
PROCESS SHOT: see CHROMA KEY
PROPS: objects used for set decoration, etc.
PTV: Public Television. See ETV.
QUICK STUDY: ANNCR who learns script and action fast
RACK: to move camera in or out, up or down
RASTER: a sort of graph-like pattern on a SCOPE with technical information that the home receiver uses in translating the electronic signals into picture and sound
REVERB: reverberation, a kind of echo effect which gives the voice or sound more "presence" as if in a concert hall or a room which has not been deadened to prevent echo, as studios are. Not the same as ECHO FX or ECHO RETURN, which is like a real echo, but can be drawn out electronically (ATTENUATED or ATTEN)
RISER: small platform to make something higher or somebody taller
REEL: the spool that tape or film is wound on
RP: rear screen projection, now accomplished by CK (CHROMA KEY)
SAG: Screen Actors Guild. A union, same as AFTRA. Some ANNCRS belong to one, some to the other, some to both. Rates are pretty much the same
SEG: Screen Extras Guild (union)
SERVO LENS: part of zoom system
SHOT: any uninterrupted, unedited sequence
SESAC: Society of European Stage Authors and Composers. A copyright service that collects royalties
SEGUE: in radio, dissolve from one sound to another

SINCERE SHOT: MCU, medium closeup
SLATE: an actual slate on which is chalked identifying date: advertiser, agency, date, take length and title of commercial. It is taped at the beginning of the spot
SET: everything the camera sees except the ANNCR
SHADING: adjusting picture contrast
SIG: like a logo, but usually a musical FX. A very short MUSIC FX is called a STINGER
SLIDE: just like the ones you take with your camera; used interchangeably with film, tape. Most studios have a SLIDE CHAIN, a camera permanently attached to a slide projector

STILL: photograph, printed on paper, not slide or transparency
SMPTE: Society of Motion Picture and Television Engineers (union)
SNOW: interference on screen, looks like snow
SOF: sound on film; not silent film
SOT: sound on tape
STORYBOARD: picture-and-caption treatment of copy
STRIKE: dismantle set
SUPER: superimpose
SWITCHBACK: cross out
SWITCHER: panel that switches cameras, sound, FX
SYNC: synchronization of picture and sound impulses. Used with many technical procedural terms that do not concern the writer, such as SYNC GEN, SYNC PULSE, etc. Included here only so you will not be intimidated by them when you are in a studio
SPOT: commercial
TAKE: a trial taping of a commercial, numbered so you can identify a particular "take" as the one you like best, as in "That's a KEEPER. Take 4 is our MASTER. Dub six copies, separate boxes, and erase the other takes." Happiest words the crew ever hears
TD: technical director
TELEPROMPTER, TELECUE: idiot sheet
TILT: rack camera up or down
TITLE DRUM: drum on which titles are rolled
TONGUE: camera movement with camera on boom

TONNAGE: practice of selling time priced per GRP—Gross Rating Point—and not telling the advertiser what each spot costs, or where it might run
TVR: obsolete, Television Recording, kine
THREE-SHOT: scene with three people; there are also TWO-SHOTS, etc.
UPCUT: sound cut off beginning or end of a commercial when broadcast, because of new, improved automated equipment which often cuts a second off the audio. So now you have to limit audio to 28½ seconds on a 30-; 58½ seconds on a 60-second commercial.
UHF: Ultra High Frequency TV: channels above 13
VHF: Very High Frequency TV: the channels 1 through 13
VIGNETTE: scene that intentionally fades at edges
VIEWFINDER: small TV screen on camera that the cameraman looks at
VTR: Videotape Recording
WIPE: FX where one picture appear to wipe over, or peel off to reveal another
ZOOM: pushing in or pulling back from subject. Same as DOLLY except that it is done with a ZOOM LENS (ZOOMAR) instead of moving the camera, hence it is faster
ZILCH: zero. A commercial the client did not buy anything, nothing accomplished

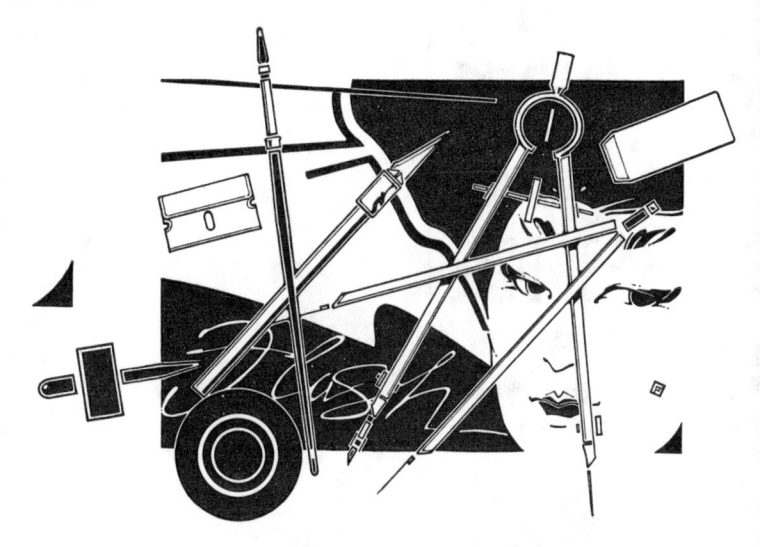

Example One:

Dat. #1 Dlr.

IN SOUTHERN CALIFORNIA
'72, '73, '74, '75, '76, '77, '78
AWARD OF MERIT WINNER

MORRIE SAGE'S UNIVERSAL CITY DATSUN

OPEN TILL 10 P.M.
EVERY DAY INCL. SAT & SUN.

PARTS & SERVICE OPEN
SATURDAYS TILL 6 P.M.
WEEKDAYS TILL 8 P.M.

YOU WILL NEVER KNOW

if you got the
BEST DEAL
ON YOUR DATSUN
unless
you check with the
#1

DATSUN DEALER SINCE 1972
IN SOUTHERN CALIFORNIA

OVER 75 Z's

TO CHOOSE FROM
Including: NEW
'79 280-ZX's

Many with Grand Luxury Pkgs.
240's-260's-280's
2+2's & COUPES
4 speeds, 5 speeds, automatics

OVER
400 Datsuns
FOR
$ALE

WE WILL TRY TO ARRANGE THE
C-R-E-D-I-T
to meet most financial conditions
& also save you money!
Drive home today
in the car of your choice

Universal City Datsun

LOCATED ON THE
Hollywood Freeway
GET OFF AT THE
Lankershim Bl.—Universal City
OFF-RAMP in North Hollywood
turn left & you're there.
AREA CODE (213)
769-8100
★★★★★★

COPY

Client:

Title:

Date: Length:

LIST OF SOUND EFFECTS:

Car Skid
Car Skid and crash
Car Sequence
Car stops, engine idles
Car door closes
Car horn
Throaty car horn
Traffic
Bus
Motorcycle
Truck
Tractor
Vacuum Cleaner
Water Pours Into Glass
Pop Bottle Sequence
Washing Machine
Bath Being Drawn
Shower
Tea Kettle Sequence
Lawnmower, Hand type
Children Playing in School
Baby Cries
Telephone Rings Five Times
Telephone Sequence #1
Telephone Sequence #2
Telephone Busy Signal
Carnival Midway
Shooting Gallery
Roller Coaster
Parade, Marching Band
Bowling Sequence
Bowling Alleys
Sports Car Race
Horse Race
Door Buzzer
Door Chimes
Door Knocks
Key in Lock
Door Opens and Closes Quickly
Door Opens and Closes

Coyote Howls
Horse Whinnies
Squeaky Water Pump
Chopping Wood
Milking Machine
Gong, One Stroke
Gong, Seven Strokes
Cuckoo Clock Strikes
Big Ben Strikes Twelve
Small Clock Ticking
Ticking, Then Alarm
Alarm Only
Grandfather clock
School Bell
News Presses
City Room
Teletypes
Linotype Machine
Busy Office Area
Standard Typewriter
IBM Electric Typewriter
Cash Register
Adding Machine Sequence
Calculator
4-Engine Piston
4-Engine Piston
Spad (World War I
World War II Fighter
707 Jet Take Off
707 Jet Landing
Piston Airliner Landing
F-100 Jet Fighter Take
F-100 Sub Sonic Fly By
F-100 Sonic Boom
Multi-Engine Piston
Rocket Countdown
Expectant Crowd Noise
Applauding Audience
Cafeteria Background

SPOT BROADCASTING ORDER

TO: ORDER #:

DATE:

PLEASE BROADCAST ADVERTISING OF:

LENGTH OF BROADCAST	HOUR	DAYS	PROGRAM	TIMES PER WEEK

DATE OF FIRST BROADCAST	EXPIRATION DATE

PROGRAM MATERIAL ARRANGEMENTS

COPY	KEY

ADDITIONAL INSTRUCTIONS

COST

LESS AGENCY COMMISSION _____ ON GROSS

YOU ARE SPECIFICALLY PROHIBITED FROM BROADCASTING THIS MATERIAL OR FURNISHING ANY DUPLICATE TAPES, ET'S OR ANY COPY OF THIS MATERIAL TO ANYONE WITHOUT PRIOR PERMISSION OF THIS AGENCY.

For a complete list of sound effects and media music write:
Capital Records
Hollwood and Vine
Hollwood, California 90028
(213) 462-6252

Make sure to ask for MEDIA MUSIC No. 14

CHAPTER TWELVE

QUICK RELIEF FOR YOUR MONEY PROBLEMS

The guys who have made it big in mail order publishing do not hide their accomplishments or themselves under bushel baskets. Every time we pick up a magazine or newspaper we see their names and advertisements. Their names read like a Mail Order Who's Who:

Jerry Buchanan	Melvin Powers
John Chriswell	Robert Ringer
Daniel A. Crandall	Robert Shindler
Dean Du Vall	Ben Swarze
Joe Karbo(d)	Mike Warren
Debra A. Grubbs	Bud Weckesser
Paul Michael	

They're all mail order legends and have pocketed fortunes.

Surprisingly, these generous mail order legends are more than willing to share their secrets of success. There are no locked vaults or armed security guards keeping their success stories or methods hidden. Actually, they are delighted to tell you how they made their millions by selling published materials through the mail.

And unlike the master chef who gives you his famous recipe but leaves out an important ingredient or cheats a little on the amount of an ingredient, you'll find no missing ingredients here. Among the things they'll tell you are:

What is Mail Order	Ad Costs
Selling Through Direct Mail	Testing Your Ads
How to Choose a Subject	Where You Should Advertise
Evaluating a Successful Subject	Developing Your Market
Art Work	Direct Mail Packages
Staying On the Legal Side	Selling Through Agents
Testing Your Market	Postage Shortcuts
Writing Ads That Sell	Finding the Perfect Printer
Copywriters	Filling Your Orders
Buying Lists	Keeping Records
Compiling Lists	Using An Ad Agency
Selling Through Follow-up	Setting Up Your Ad Agency
How to Set Your Price	Copyrights
Guarantees	Calculating Your Cost

But as you read and absorb these and other chapters, suddenly it doesn't seem so easy. All the elements covered in these books can be overwhelming to the novice. It's literally too much for the little guy to comprehend all at once. It's enough to make him give up the whole idea.

This would be a big mistake. The truth is that most successful entrepreneurs knew absolutely nothing about the business of mail order selling when they started and they started with very small initial investments. It's easy to lose track of this fact when you're midway through their books and under an avalanche of information.

Mail order publishing is definitely a business which can be started with nearly nothing. It's a business you can learn as you go along and a business that is continually opening up new horizons of publication possibilities. Best of all for a newcomer, it can still be started on a shoestring and with only a knowledge of the basic steps it can lead to the beginner's name joining that respected list of entrepreneurs who have made fortunes in mail order publishing.

SELECTING YOUR SUBJECT

The most important element for the little guy just starting out is to have a marketable product, one that can be produced at a minimum expense and that will sell inexpensively to the public. The solution is to sell information. If you know a great deal about a particular subject that can help others, people will pay you for this information. Surveys have proved that people are most interested in three subjects: health, sex and beauty. If you can tell them something they don't already know or help them in any of these areas, you're nearly guaranteed a big seller your first time at bat.

People desperately want to be healthy and to live as long as possible. And folks can't seem to get enough information on sex. Look at the covers of all the magazines at your favorite newsstand. Count the number of articles relating to sex which get cover space. You'll be amazed at the wide range of magazines that know this topic sells and utilize it in one manner or another to increase the sales pull of that month's issue.

Beauty is as big a sales puller as sex. Men, Women and Teen magazines concentrate an exhorbitant amount of space on this subject. Physical fitness is a big part of being beautiful. Also count the number of magazines at your newsstand which are devoted just to beauty. Everyone wants to improve their appearance. Tell people how to achieve this improvement and they'll rush to send you their money.

If you haven't discovered the diet that lets you eat all you want of your favorite foods and lose ten pounds a week, discovered the key to being the perfect lover, really discovered the fountain of youth or found the magic formula that will turn ugly ducklings into beautiful swans, don't dispair. There are plenty of other topics people will pay money to learn more about.

"How-to" information is extremely popular. People want to know how to renovate old houses and how to get the best buy on a new one. They want to know how to make money, save money, invest money and how to spend it wisely. They want to know how to pay the least amount of taxes, how to get along better with people, how to garden and enjoy hobbies, how to do household maintenance chores, how to fix their cars and how to get along with their spouses or, in the event they can't, how to divorce them as cheaply as possible. The list of how-to articles you can publish is endless. One of the most successful mail order publishers, Jerry Buchanan, actually started his business with a 700-word report on how to get rid of moles and gophers!

If you aren't an expert on any subject, become one. Select a subject you believe will appeal to a mass audience. Then go to the library. Read everything you can find on your topic: books, reference materials and encyclopedias. Ask the librarian to show you how to find and use the newspaper and periodical indexes which list every article printed on your topic. Learn to use the microfilm machines to check the features printed in back issues of newspapers, especially the *New York Times,* and back issues of magazine articles on your subject. Learn everything you can about this topic.

If your topic is one that requires a skill, go watch the procedure in progress. Talk to the person who does it. Find out how he learned to do it and everything about each step of the procedure. Take step-by-step pictures and write down each detail. Be specific. Omit nothing. Even learn to do it. When you're finished with your research, you should not only know what you're talking about, but be expert enough to tell others *exactly* how to do it.

Don't dispair if you can't find much material on your subject in the library. This is not a negative. It's a sure sign that your topic is fresh and not one which has already saturated the marketplace. This makes it an even more marketable mail order product.

If there isn't any readily available information on your topic, how are you going to become an expert? Easily. You're going to become an investigative reporter. Start by checking the Yellow Pages for stores, shops or businesses where you can learn more about your topic. Call and interview the managers of these operations. Like a reporter, ask questions and more questions. Talk to as many people as you can find who know anything at all about your topic and don't forget to ask each of them if they know anyone else who can give you information. Follow every lead. Sometimes all you'll have to start with is a short article in your local newspaper about a new product, an idea on a how-to subject or even a sales ad. Track down the reporter and call the name in the ad. Most people are flattered to talk to a reporter or writer and will be extremely open and frank.

Don't give up until you've got all the information you'll need. All your investigating and researching will pay off. In mail order publishing usually the more difficult it is to track your information, the better the topic. If your information is truly fresh and new and you're the only person with it, your sales will soar!

WRITING YOUR REPORT

Now that you've done your research and become an expert, it's time to write your first how-to report. How long should it be? It should always be long enough to impart every detail of your information but still be as short as possible. Your first reports should run no more than two single-spaced typewritten pages printed on both sides. That's the equivalent of four pages or approximately 2800 words. Keep this space allocation in mind when you choose a topic. If you can contain your report to one page, that's even better. The more pages it takes for you to relay your information, the greater your printing costs. Nowhere is "just the facts" more important than in writing mail order how-to informational reports.

Use a friendly, straightforward writing style, but be specific and concise. Never use two words when one word will do. You have information to impart and frankly that's all the reader is interested in. Don't try to impress him with big words or your intellectual level. He's not interested in either. He just wants facts. Give them to him in a quick, uncomplicated manner and he'll be a satisfied customer.

Do keep your dictionary handy. There's no excuse for misspelled words and you'll quickly lose your reader's respect if your report is peppered with them. Also heed your grammar. No one is going to take a red pencil to your report like your sixth grade English teacher, but do avoid glaring errors. A copy of *The Elements of Style* by William Strunk, Jr. and E. B. White will cost you $1.65 at your bookstore and save you from most noticeable grammatical errors.

If you feel that you can't possibly write your own report, don't just quit. You can still make your fortune in mail order publishing. The success of your business does not depend on your writing ability. You can still get into this business and make the kind of money you've only dreamed about before without writing a single word of your own.

There are free reports available to you just for the asking. The largest publisher of information in the world is the United States Government. It prints informational and how-to brochures, reports and books. Write to the U.S. Government Printing Office, Superintendent of Documents, P.O. Box 1821, Washington, DC 20402 for a free copy of their catalog. Also request that your name be placed on their mailing list. Much of this material is absolutely free. Others are reasonably priced. It's also Not copyrighted and you can republish it as printed. It's perfectly legal. However, for the respect of your peers and customers, it is advisable to rewrite the material in your own style.

You can also hire a freelance writer to write your report for you. It will add to your initial investment but not as much as you may think. Just look under Writers in the Yellow Pages of your telephone book. Also check Writer's Agents and Writer's Organizations. Most organizations have directories and can recommend an appropriate writer to prepare your report.

An excellent place to find a good freelance writer is in your small local weekly newspaper. Just because writers are writing in small publications doesn't mean they aren't good writers. Often they're beginners earning the credits that will open the door for them in larger newspapers. Sometimes they're retired writers just keeping their foot in the door or women, former full-time writers who are now at home with small children but are practicing their craft part time.

These writers work for low fees. Usually they do all their own research and interviewing and are not reimbursed for their expenses. They are usually paid between $15 to $25 for a 1000-word article. That's an average of 2 cents per word. You should have no problem getting one of these writers to take on your already researched project. At 2 cents per word your maximum 2800-word article will cost you $56.

Be sure you explain in detail to your writer exactly how you want your report written. If you have a copy of a report written in the style you are seeking, show it to your writer. The clearer your instructions as to how you want the article written, the better chance you have of getting the job done right and without the necessity of a rewrite.

But whether you write your report or have it written, copyright it. The copyright law states that you own the copyright to your material for 50 years or until you sell your rights to the material. But stealing does occur in this business. It will only cost you $10 and two copies of your manuscript to protect yourself. Call or write the Copyright Office, Library of Congress, Washington, DC 20559 for a booklet covering this subject. If you've employed a freelance writer, be certain to get a contract stating that the work was for hire and that the writer has sold all rights to the report to you.

SELLING YOUR REPORT

One of the most important elements of your venture is selling your report. A classified advertisement is your cheapest and most advisable method at this point. The big guys can afford to write several different full page ads, offer their material at various prices, and test their pull in several different publications. The little guy can't afford this procedure at this point in his operation.

Start your mail order selling locally. If you have a bi-monthly community newspaper, check its rates and circulation. You want to reach as many people as possible for your money. A circulation of 50,000 usually charges 50 cents per word. So a 20-word ad will cost you $10 per issue. However, the longer you run your ad the less per word you pay. Also, it's a proven fact that ads should run at least three issues for you to be able to make a fair judgment of their capability.

Tabloid newspapers, familiar at your local grocery checkout counters, are a big market for classified advertising. Their circulations are huge. The *Star,* for instance, has a circulation of 3.75 million per week. Its rates are:

$5.80 per word per one issue

$5.60 per word per four or more issues

A minimum ad is ten words.

A 20-word classified ad running four times will cost you $112.00.

Money and circulation should not be your only consideration when choosing a publication for your ad. The big boys test their ads by running them in several different publications before they invest large advertising dollars in the more expensive publications. Three or four smaller newspapers will usually give them a feel for how the public is going to respond to their ad. Keep this in mind. You may not have the funds to properly test your ad but by starting small and working your way up you have a built-in testing situation. If you discover immediately that your ad pulls little response in comparison to the circulation, then you've learned that it will have to be improved before your graduate to a larger and more expensive publication.

No matter how informative your report, it's a failure if no one reads it. This is where your "salesman" comes in. In mail order your "salesman" is your classified ad. It is the key to your success or failure.

Study every classified ad you can find, but pay special attention to those ads which will be your competitors. Expand your search to magazines and include those aimed at the entrepreneur or individual looking for money-making opportunities. Cut out the ads that catch your eye. Note what they say with minimum wording. These are attention getters and this is the kind of ad you want to write.

Don't miss checking the tabloids. These ads reach a vast number of people and are responsible for a large amount of mail order sales. Study these classifieds closely. Obtain back copies of the tabloids from friends, neighbors; anywhere you can get them. If you can get copies several months old, your survey will be that much more revealing and rewarding. Ads which disappear quickly obviously were not well written or advertising a desirable product. Those which appear month after month are obvious winners. These are models for the type of ad you want to sell your informational report.

But do not copy these ads. Seek freshness and originality. There are a lot of ads and reading them can become boring to the potential customer. Yours must be an eye-catcher and different!

Send for the free detail packages offered in the classified ads. Study these packages when you receive them. Note everything; label, envelope, colors, art work, graphics, paper quality. Invest in a few of your competitors' how-to offers.

At $1 to $3 each you can afford to buy quite a few. You can't be competitive if you don't know what your competition is offering.

Practice writing your ad over and over. If you have to write 100 ads to get one really good, super "salesman," then write that many. It's not easy but you can write a classified ad that will bring in profits.

DIRECT MAIL

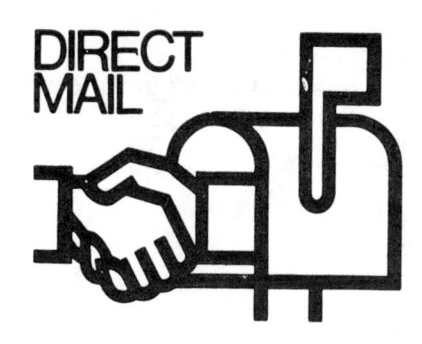

This ad must include your product and why the buyer will be better off after purchasing it. It must also include your name and address. Use only your initials with your last name to save space. You must also include your price and a guarantee. Mail order buyers suspect any publisher who doesn't guarantee his product or offer a full refund. All of this must fit into only four lines if you're to keep your advertising dollars within your limited budget.

Another decision you'll have to make is whether to use your home address or a post office box. A small post office box will cost you about $7 per year, but, of course, you'll want a large one to hold all your orders—$12 per year. There are indications that some mail order buyers place more trust in a business type address than they do in an ad listing just a name and post office box number. There are no definite statistics proving one way will actually result in a major profit difference. This choice is up to you but a business name with address just might pull a little bit better. Or you can compromise. Use a title such as your last name plus the word "Publications" and a post office box.

If writing your own classified ad is too overwhelming, and it is for many people, even professional writers, invest in a good copywriter. One experienced in mail order selling is your best bet. Use the same methods you used for finding your freelance writer. You can also call the Direct Mail Marketing Association at (212) 689-4977 and have them recommend several copywriters in your area. In addition you can call fund-raising organizations and ask if they will recommend a good freelance copywriter. They usually have a list on file. Small advertising agencies also use freelancers and will share a name or two with you.

But good copywriters do not come cheap. Unless you can do it yourself, and do a really good job at it, it should be considered a vital investment. Here are three suggestions for good copywriters:

Stephen Nevard
49 Quinnipiac Plaza, Suite H
North Haven, CT 06473

John Francis Tighe
72 West 85th St.
New York, NY 10024

Luther Brock
2911 Nottingham
Denton, TX 76201

Keep in mind that you are not just looking for a copywriter to prepare your first classified ad. You're entering the mail order publishing business and just around the corner you're going to need a complete direct mail package. This includes letters, brochures, envelopes and return order cards. Mail order publishers do not get rich off of one how-to report. That's only the beginning.

Interview your prospective copywriters by phone and ask them to send samples of their direct mail order packages. In addition to this copywriter composing your first ad, you'll need him or her to write a flyer advertising your next report to be included with every one of your first-sold reports. That's right. When you finish your first report, you can't just sit back on your accomplishment. You want to make money and making money means taking advantage of every opportunity. In this case, repeat sales to customers is your gold mine.

In every order package you want to include an advertisement selling your next report. This flyer should be as colorful and graphically designed as you can afford. It is another "salesman" calling on your new customer. Also included with the flyer should be an order card for the customer's convenience. All the customer should have to do is check "yes" on the card and mail it back to you. You're now selling your second report, even without the benefit of another classified ad. Of course, you'll follow later with a classified ad for this new report just as soon as your profits from report number one permit.

How will you know how good your classified ad is and if your copywriter has done the job for you? Unfortunately you won't know right away. You'll have to wait until all the results are in from your ad. In a daily newspaper you'll know in three weeks. You should give the ad that much time. Bimonthly newspapers and weekly tabloids will take longer and monthly magazines even longer because of the time lapse before your ad appears and starts to draw. If it's running over several weekly issues or monthly issues, the time frame will be even longer.

But you can know in advance how many orders you will have to fill to break even on your ad costs. For instance, if your ad costs $65.76 and you sell your report for $2, you simply divide the ad cost by your gross and you immediately know that your break-even ad cost point is 33 orders. If the ad doesn't make that figure, forget it and reevaluate your report. If you still believe in it, then write a new ad or get your copywriter to rewrite it or get yourself a new copywriter.

When your success is evident and you've made a good profit, your copywriter should design a direct mail package for you to use in selling your expanded line of how-to reports. It should be included in every new order you ship. The more marketable reports you have available, the more opportunity you have to make more money.

As you grow you'll need your copywriter even more. You'll need more direct mail packages to sell your brochures, booklets, newsletters, and your ultimate goal, books. Good copywriting, whether yours or an employee's, can make the difference between your mail order business being mildly successful or a whooping success.

PRICING YOUR REPORT

Pricing your report is also of major importance. I have found that buyers do not respond well to odd prices, such as $2.98 or $3.85. They respond much better to even prices, such as $1, $2, or $3. In addition, fewer refunds are reported at these prices than at odd prices or higher prices.

Determining your report price depends on your expenses. Add all your expenses: what it cost to research your report, advertising charges, printing costs, mailing packaging and postage. If you decided to use a post office box, include this expense. A good, complete expenditure report wil even include the costs of opening new bank accounts and writing checks.

If you've done all the writing yourself, you'll probably be able to produce and mail each report for as little as 25 cents. Always work on a 200 to 400 percent markup for your informational and how-to reports. Price your reports at $2 or $4, depending on your expenditures, how fresh the information is and the demand you expect for it.

Of course, if you've used professional writers, it will take a bite out of your profits. Go for as high a markup as possible with a $5 price. Try to maintain at least a 200 percent markup or better. If you don't you won't succeed in making the kind of money you're seeking. It will also take you longer to build your mail order publishing business into a big success. Once you're a success, using professional writers and copywriters won't have as big an impact on your profits—they'll actually be responsible for raising them—but in the beginning they may cause you to have to exercise a little more patience before your fortune is realized.

You don't have to invest money in printing your reports prior to running your ad. You can wait for your ad to appear and the orders to begin pouring in. Earlier you will, of course, have visited several printers to learn exactly what they can do for you and how much it's going to cost you to print your report and advertising flyer. Take time to talk to them about your future direct mail package plans too. Show them your report on your first visit and samples of how you want your report to look. Make certain the printer understands you want quality work but that your budget is a major consideration at this time.

Each printer is different and each has his own way of doing things. They also vary in price. Choose the printer who guides you to the best quality work at a fair price. Also ask about time frame for completing your job. Some printers will advertise 24-hour service but don't expect a job of your size to be done that quickly. Allow at least five days for the printer to complete your work.

So how many of your first reports and second sales approaches and reorder cards do you order? The price per piece goes down with the higher quantity you purchase. Watch your mail box. U.S. Government regulations require that mail order purchases be shipped within 30 days, so you have a good week to a week and a half to see the orders start coming in. Then you can judge quantity, place your order at the printer's and get the best price. But then ship immediately. If you aren't cutting your profit margin too close, you can order your projected printing needs before then and still get the same quantity pricing. Also you'll be shipping sooner and your customers will note your quick return.

BUILDING YOUR MAILING LIST

You must keep meticulous records and I don't just mean bookkeeping. Maintaining a list of your customers is one of the most important elements of your mail order publishing business. Write the customer's name, address, zip code, what he purchased, and the date on a 3x5 card and file it. Each of your first customers should recieve with his order a flyer and order card selling your second report. As they reorder pull this card and record this new sale. Establish a new file for these dual customers. Enclosed in their second order, of course, is a sales package for your third report. Now you're getting the feel for how it works. You keep mailing to your reordering customers, then send to your next best prospects on file and periodically to those who only buy infrequently.

Now you're also in the list-building business. You're constructing your own collection of mail order buyers. This list will serve you three ways: you're more likely to sell to these proven mail order buyers; you will increase your sales; and later when you've collected thousands of names, you can rent them to other mail order business houses or brokers. The fee is about $65 per one thousand names. List renting can add a healthy increase to your profits. And don't forget, while you're utilizing your lists, you're also collecting new customers by continually running your classified ads.

COUNTING YOUR PROFITS

So how do you figure your profits? It's quite simple. You add all your expenditures and then subtract them from the total dollars you receive. The difference is your profit.

For instance, let's assume your first project cost you $.40 each and your instincts and research told you to price it at $4. Your classified ad appeared in National Enquirer so you received only 500 inquires and sold 17 percent. But with a 1000 percent markup you made $340 profit on this first small effort. Imagine if you had ten reports circulating at one time under the same circumstances. That's $3,400. See the possibilities of making big money?

For now, you're still a little guy but you've got the chance to get a little bigger. You've got $340 to push your next report and expand your advertising to more than just your one previous source. But when you advertise in more than one publication, be certain to key your ad. In each publication, have one thing—a letter or number—different in your name or address so you'll be able to identify from which ad you receive each order. This way you'll know which publication and which ad are pulling the most orders for you. Those ads which aren't pulling will be just as visible. You'll quickly discover where to place particular subjects for the best sales results and where you'll get the most for each of your advertising dollars.

Keep putting your profits back into your business. Bigger customer lists and more ads equal more sales. It won't be long until you'll have parlayed your meager beginning into a publishing business that can expand into books. Then you'll be able to afford those full-page advertisements that result in million-dollar profits.

Now you're no longer a little guy. Your first book can even be the tale of your own business success. You can write your own books and rake in all of the profits or hire writers to write them for you. You can also purchase books that are written and aimed for mail order sales. The following publishers will supply you with mail order best sellers:

Wholesale Book Corporation
902 Broadway
New York, NY 10010

Associated Booksellers
147 McKinley Avenue
Bridgeport, CT 06606

Book Sales, Inc.
110 Enterprise Avenue
Secaucus, NJ 07094

Some wholesale publishing houses will even drop-ship orders for you, saving you storage space.

When you look at mail order publishing from the first easy step and follow the process one step at a time, it no longer appears overwhelming or impossible. It is neither. If you're willing to take it slowly, learn and grow as you produce, and keep plowing your profits back into your business, you've got everything it takes to have your name added to that list of legends who've made millions in mail order publishing.

The following is a list of ideal publications for selling books by mail:
(Write to them for a free copy of their publication and a classified ad rate card.)

Moneysworth
251 W. 57th St.
New York, NY 10019
(212) 581-2000

Salesman's Opportunity
6 N. Michigan Ave. Suite 1405
Chicago, Ill. 60602
(312) 346-4790

Specitaly Salesman
6285 Barfield Road
Atlanta, GA. 30328
(404) 393-2920

Spare Time
919 N. Michigan Ave.
Chicago, Ill. 60611
(312) 787-4545

Success Unlimited
401 N. Wabash Ave.
Chicago, Ill. 60611
(312) 828-9500

Financial Opportunities
4035 W. Dempster St.
Skokie, Ill. 60076
(312) 679-3255

Wall Street Journal
22 Cortlandt St.
New York, NY 10007
(212) 285-5000

Workbench
4251 Pennsylvania Ave.
Kansas City, MO. 64111
(816) 531-5730

Firehouse
515 Madison Ave.
New York, NY 10022
(212) 935-4553

Official Detective Group
235 Park Ave.
New York, NY 10003
(212) 777-0800

Keystone Motorist
2040 Market St.
Philadelphia, PA. 19103
(215) 864-5455

Michigan Living Motor News
Auto Club Dr.
Dearborn, MI. 48126
(313) 336-1516

Minnesota AAA Motorist
7 Travelers Trail
Burnsvill, MN. 55337
(612) 890-2300

National Motorist
1 Market Plaza Suite 300
San Francisco, CA. 94105
(415) 777-4000

New York Motorist
28 E. 78 St.
New York, NY 10021
(212)586-1166

Ohio Motorist
P.O. Box 6150
Cleveland, OH. 44101
(216) 579-6236

Consumer Life
1999 Shepard Rd.
St. Paul, MN. 55116
(612) 647-7238

Family Weekly
641 Lexington Ave.
New York, NY 10022
(212) 980-0300

Parade
750 Third Ave.
New York, NY 10017
(212) 573-7000

Saturday Evening Post
1100 Waterway Blvd.
Indianapolis, IN.
(317) 634-1100

Mother Earth News
105 Stoney Mtn Rd.
Hendersonville, NC 28739
(704) 693-0211

New York Times Magazine
229 W. 57th St.
New York, NY 10036
(212) 556-1201

Psychology Today
One Park Ave.
New York, NY 10016
(212) 725-3995

Spotlight
300 Independence Ave.
Washington, DC 20003
(202) 546-3787

Writer's Digest
9933 Alliance Rd.
Cincinnati, OH 45242
(513) 984-0717

Americal Way
488 Madison Ave.
New York, NY 10022
(212) 826-9453

Eastern Review
5900 Wilishire Blvd.
Los Angeles, CA. 90036
(213) 937-5810

Pan Am Clipper
One Park Ave
New York, NY 10016
(212) 725-7221

Penthouse
909 Third Ave.
New York, NY 10022
(212) 593-3301

Playboy
747 Third Ave.
New York, NY 10017
(212) 688-3030

Signature
880 Third Ave.
New York, NY 10022
(212) 888-9450

Sky
99 N.W. 183rd St.
Miami, Fla. 33169
(305) 865-2661

Smithsonian
420 Lexington Ave.
New York, NY 10017
(212) 490-2510

Travel Leisure
1350 Avenue of the Americas
New York, NY 10019
(212) 399-2553

"Are The Banks, Insurance Companies, and the U.S. Government Keeping $20 Billion Dollars Of Your Money?"

"Are The Banks, Insurance Companies, and the U.S. Government Keeping $20 Billion Dollars Of Your Money?"

Your father, mother, Grand father, Grand mother, uncle, second cousin or some lost relative may have left you a fortune.

This fabulous and little-known sum of money is made up of unclaimed or forgotten Estates, Savings Deposits, Checking Accounts, Stocks, Dividends, Insurance Polices, State Government Bonds.

Although millions of dollars have been found for seventy-thousand people, the majority of unclaimed dollars ($20 Billion) grows every year be at least another billion dollars. This unclaimed money has attracted the attention of every state government. They have introduced into law ways of taking over the money from banks, courts, insurance companies and corporations that have been holding it. Most state governments take the money and hold it for eventual claimers.

Millions of people could claim their inheritance, if they only knew they were heirs and if they could be found. It is for sure that most state governments aren't very anxious to find the missing claimants to his or her lost estate.

Why are there so many missing heirs and so much unclaimed money?

To begin with, there is NO Central, national registration of all unclaimed or abandoned sums.

Here are some other factors too. We live in a fast moving country. Millions of families change residence every year. Many fail to leave accurate change of mailing addresses; some fail to leave any. Most of us do, but the post office only retains such records for one year.

I figure that one out of every fifteen Americans has some money awaiting him that he know or she knows nothing about. You could easly be one of them. Your money, or the records pertaining to it, may be in some obscure vault, lawyer's file, or a dusty ledger in some bank. It might not be much, two or three thousand, but it also could be a considerable fortune: some $7,000,000 in one case.

In any case that money ought to be in your pocket right now. You could be spending it, investing it, living high on it. It's yours.

Here's how you go about finding out if you have any lost money coming to you.

There are two tracing companies in the United States who for a fee will find out if you have any lost money coming to you.

Markham Research Company
39 Broadway
New York, NY 10017

Missing Heirs International
11 West 44th Street
New York, NY 10036

If you would like to try and trace your own fortune. I suggest that you write to the Insurance companies and Banks listed. They have records going back to the early 1900's.

What you will need to provide them with is a list of your relatives on both sides of your family tree going back as far as you can. (To the early 1900's if possible.) You need to list you Grand father, Grand mother, Great Grand Father, Great Grand Mother. All aunts, sisters, uncles second cousins, thrid cousins, fourth cousins, and so on. As many as you can remember. You must also list any former addresses you may know of, for the members of your family.

1. Keep the letter short.
2. Enclose a self-addressed, stamped envelope for reply.
3. DO NOT send it certified or registered mail. It will be refused.

It's the Markham Company who is the new tracing company on the block.

The Markham Company is one of a few companies that specialize in tracing people who don't know, or don't remember, that they own securities. Companies like Coca-Cola Co. and Xerox Corp. don't like being saddled with unclaimed stocks or money. By law, companies must turn over dormant stocks and monies to state governments or face legal penalties; from public-relations stand-point, they would much rather see the stocks back in the hands of their rightful owners.

Since 1960, Markham says it has renunited more than 50,000 people with nearly $25 Million dollars in unclaimed securities. The recipients-often the spouses or descendants of long-dead shareholders- must agree to pay The Markham Company 30% to 50% of the find's value before learning what the securities are now worth.

Markham's staff of 35 uses the Library of Congress, old phone books, and private investigators to reunite people with their holdings. About 70% of the time, staff members say, they find the person they're after, even through the passing of years can make it diffcult.

A few years ago, Markham tracked down the grandson of an Englishman who had bought stock in a Canadian mining company nearly 80 years earlier. The stock brought for $1,200 was worth $300,000. In another case, U.S. Steel Corp. asked Markham to trace some unclaimed securities worth $175,000; after three years, Markham found a 90-year old woman In West Germany whose husband had brought the stock decades earlier in the U.S., then returned home to West Germany where he died in a concentration camp during World War II.

The following people may have money waiting for them:

Isaac Hecht (heirs of)	New York City	80,000
Helen Hegnauer	Miami, FL	48,700
Olga Helin (Mrs)	Mount Vernon, New York	222,400
John Helmke	Brooklyn, New York	16,000
Christine Henderson	Newport, CA	67,200
Joseph Herbick	New York City	159,000
Jose Penalver Hernandez	Long Beach, CA	4,500
George Hey	Washington, DC	86,900
Annie Higgins	Orange, New Jersey	6,600
Helen M.J. Hogan	Long Island City, New York	7,000
Richard Hogan	Portland, Main	5,700
Milly Honchier	New York, NY	4,000
Agnes Hope	Chicago, ILL	4,400
Edward Hopkins	Portland, OR	18,000
John Horigan	Jackson, Miss	10,000
Fred Howart	Youngstown, OH	9,700
Elijah H. Hunt	Trenton, New Jersey	7,1000
Sheila Hurley (Miss)	Los Angles, CA	1,1150
Jacob S. Hursh	Lafayette, New Jersey	6,500
Nora Hynes	San Francisco, CA	4,400
William Irving	Newark, New Jersey	6,500

This is just a small list of people who may have money waiting for them.

Insurance Companies:

Bankers Life Company
6404 Wilshire Blvd
Los Angeles, CA

CNA Insurance
600 S. Commonwealth Ave.
Los Angeles, CA

Geico Insurance Co.
2120 Wisconsin Ave.
Washington, DC

Colonial Penn Insurance
315 Arden Ave.
Glendale, CA

Farmers Insurance Group
3041 Cochran Street
Los Angeles, CA

Hartford Insurance
Hartford Plaza
Chicago, Ill.

Franklin Life Insurance
2 Northfield Plaza
Chicago, Ill

Home Insurance Company
10 S. Riverside Plaza
Chicago, Ill.

Kemper Insurance Co.
20 N. Wacker Dr.
Chicago, Ill

The Travelers Insurance Co.
100 E. 42nd Street
New York, NY

USF&G Insurance
111 Fulton Street
New York, NY

Unity Mutual Life
One Unity Plza
New York, NY

Washington Nation Life
500 5th Avenue
New York, NY

The Following are the banks that may have money waiting for you.

East New York Saving Bank
1114 Avenue of Americas
New York, NY

Dime Bank
Madison Ave. & 56th Street
New York, NY

Citibank
399 Park Ave.
New York, NY

Chemical Bank
20 Pine Street
New York, NY

Dollar Saving Bank
445 Park Ave.
New York, NY

Anchor Savings Bank
404 5th Ave.
New York, NY

Central National Bank
120 S. LaSalle
Chicago, Ill

American National Bank
33 N. LaSalle
Chicago, Ill

Continental Bank
231 S. LaSalle
Chicago, Ill

Lincoln National Bank
3959 N. Lincoln Ave.
Chicago, Ill

Crocker National Bank
333 S. Grand Ave.
Los Angeles, CA

Bank of America
3191 Wilshire Blvd.
Los Angeles, CA

© *N.S. MCMLXXXIV*